Elvis in Hawai'i

JERRY HOPKINS

BESS PRESS

3565 Harding Ave. Honolulu, Hawai'i 96816
www.besspress.com

Design: Carol Colbath and Julie Falvey

Front cover: Elvis at *Arizona* Memorial benefit concert press conference. Photo by John Lau of City Art Works, Hawai'i's first rock and roll photographer. This photograph may not be reproduced or transmitted by any means without the written permission of Mrs. John Lau.

Back cover: Elvis enjoying the surf at Waikīkī. Photo from Todd Slaughter Collection.

Index: Lee S. Motteler

Library of Congress Cataloging-in-Publication Data

Hopkins, Jerry.
  Elvis in Hawai'i / Jerry
Hopkins.
    p. cm.
  Includes illustrations.
  ISBN 1-57306-142-5
  ISBN 13: 978-1-57306-142-1
  1. Presley, Elvis, 1933-1977.
2. Hawaii - In motion pictures.
I. Title.
ML420.P96.H67 2002   782.421-dc21

Second printing in 2005
Third printing in 2007

Printed in China

Contents

Foreword

Memphis—Elvis Presley's home—is a long way from Hawai'i, even if they're both part of the USA. And maybe if things had gone differently, Elvis might have spent his life in Tennessee as just a regular citizen without ever having seen the Hawaiian Islands at all.

But things didn't go that way; they went spectacularly in another direction, making Elvis Presley an international phenomenon. And despite the physical distance that might easily have kept him from ever setting foot in the place, his life actually had some fascinating intersections with Hawai'i. The midocean islands influenced him, and he influenced them, and Hawai'i served as both the location of some career milestones and a place of relaxation.

Over the years, Elvis evolved to working in two different styles, and his Hawai'i performances incorporated both: the straight-out rock and roll that made him famous (or notorious, in his early years) and the toned-down pop music he gradually shifted to. In Hawai'i, the more raw stuff only came out in his live shows, and two of these (the USS *Arizona* Memorial benefit concert and the amazing worldwide satellite broadcast of "Elvis: Aloha from Hawaii") were of historic significance. In the meantime, his three Hawaiian films showcased ballads, novelty songs, and only some mild suggestions of rock. After the success of the first, 1961's *Blue Hawaii*, which outdid the lesser box office receipts of his two previous (and more serious) films, Elvis stayed away from anything heavy onscreen in his singing or acting. *Girls! Girls! Girls!* and *Paradise, Hawaiian Style* fit right into the lightweight mode that a colorful island setting seemed most suited for.

It wasn't all work, though. Elvis also needed somewhere to unwind, and he discovered Hawai'i was the place to do it (as millions of other vacationers agree). An ocean voyage on a passenger liner, comfortable accommodations in a luxury hotel, and shopping for souvenirs constituted some of the King's Hawaiian diversions. Although Elvis's first visits to the islands weren't particularly restful, with some mob scenes of crazed fans that approached panic, things mellowed in later years, and Elvis found friendly acceptance and some moments of peace in the islands.

The Hawai'i facet to the life story of Elvis Presley is important. And Jerry Hopkins, who knows about both Elvis and Hawai'i, is the perfect person to relate the tale in its entirety.

DeSoto Brown

Acknowledgments

Some of the material in this book appeared in a different form in my two previous Elvis biographies—the first, *Elvis: A Biography,* published in 1972 by Simon and Schuster, the sequel, *Elvis: The Final Years,* by St. Martin's Press in 1980.

I again want to thank the people who contributed information about Elvis in Hawai'i when I wrote those books: Tom Moffatt; Ron Jacobs; Jordanaires Gordon Stoker, Ray Walker, Neal Matthews, and Hoyt Hawkins; Minnie Pearl; Otis Blackwell; Jerry Leiber; Mike Stoller; Marty Pasetta; Jerry Schilling; Bill Belew; Joe Guercio; John Wilkinson; Ed Parker; Linda Thompson; Ginger and Jo Alden; Kalani Simerson; Eddie Sherman; and Matt Esposito.

Several were reinterviewed for this book and new sources were added. Special thanks to Velma Fisher and her daughters Mona Roblin and Luana Brown; Charlie Ross; Todd Slaughter; Mark Castillo; Martin Nolet; and Darren Julien.

Much useful information also came from the superb two-volume biography by Peter Guralnick, *Last Train to Memphis: The Rise of Elvis Presley* and *Careless Love: The Unmaking of Elvis Presley.* Internet Web sites too numerous to list also contributed much detail.

For the visual material, I'm indebted to the many individuals who contributed memorabilia to *Elvis in Hawai'i.* Mahalo to Tom Moffatt; DeSoto Brown; Bob Klein (kcreole1@optonline.net); Todd Slaughter; Judy Anderson; Pete and Bruno Hernandez; Sonnie Rodrigues, Jim Kelly, and Anne Harpham at the *Honolulu Advertiser*; Minnie Pearl Cancer Foundation; Charlie Ross; Velma Fisher; Eddie Sherman; Darren Julien for Entertainment Rarities; Mrs. John Lau; Clifford Inn at the State Historic Preservation Division; Jonathon Von Brana; and Michael Ochs Archives . Com.

Illustration and Photo Credits

Judy Anderson: 25 (top, bottom).

DeSoto Brown Collection: 3 (top, middle left, middle right), 5 (bottom right), 8 (top), 27, 30, 32 (top left, middle right, bottom left), 33 (middle, bottom), 34 (foreground), 38 (top, bottom), 39, 44 (background, top, bottom), 45 (background), 48, 50 (top, lower middle, bottom), 52 (bottom), 54, 58 (top, upper middle, lower middle, bottom), 59 (left, middle, right), 74.

John Lau of City Art Works: front cover.

Darren Julien for Entertainment Rarities: 21, 24, 70, 76, 78, 82 (left, right), 83, 84.

Velma Fisher: 4, 5 (top), 6 (bottom), 8 (bottom).

Hawai'i State Archives: 27.

Pete Hernandez: 5 (bottom left), 15, 34–35 (background), 38–39 (background), 47, 77 (top, bottom), 79, 80.

Honolulu Advertiser Archives: 2 (top, bottom), 3 (bottom), 6 (top), 11, 12, 13, 19, 22 (bottom), 23, 26, 47 (right), 61, 62, 66, 69, 71, 72 (left), 75 (left, right).

Bob Klein Archives: i, iii, viii, 2 (middle), 16, 20, 22 (middle), 31 (bottom left, top right), 33 (top), 35, 40, 42, 46, 47 (left), 52 (top), 53, 60, 61, 72 (right) 85 (right), 88 (right).

Michael Ochs Archives . Com: 87.

Minnie Pearl Cancer Foundation: 22 (top).

Tom Moffatt Collection: vi, 9, 10, 17, 18 (top, bottom), 57, 65, 72 (left), 75 (left, right).

Charlie Ross: 29 (top right, bottom right).

Eddie Sherman Photo Collection: 7, 63, 64.

Todd Slaughter Photo Collection: 36 (top, middle, bottom), 37 (top, upper middle, lower middle, bottom), 41, 43 (top, middle, bottom), 45, 49, 50 (upper middle), 51, 55, 56, 85 (left), 86 (left, right), 87 (right), 88 (left), back cover.

DLNR/SHPD: 2 (top), 6 (top), 11, 29 (left).

Jonathon Von Brana: 14.

v

Introduction

Elvis Presley first visited Hawai'i in 1957, after his manager, according to one version of the story, won a roll of the dice with a concert promoter. The story was later denied, but if it were true, it was a gamble that paid off over and over again, for both Elvis and the islands, as Hawai'i became Elvis's "second home"—the site for two of the most important concert performances of his career, a scenic backdrop for three films, and a favored vacation spot up to a few months before he died.

For three decades—the 1950s, the 1960s, and the 1970s—he appeared in Hawai'i, either in concert or in films, a record that no other non-Hawaiian performer has likely matched, or ever will.

Elvis was a welcome caller, a generous guest. By giving proceeds from two of his concerts—there were six in all—to prominent and worthy local charities, he won the hearts of Hawai'i's grownups. (He already had their daughters and many of their sons firmly in his grasp.) His pretty-as-a-postcard movies boosted the new state's tourism. Some of his most enduring and popular songs came from those movies. And in response to all the attention he gave Hawai'i, the public, in typical island style, didn't bother him when he was here on holiday.

Today, thousands of Elvis fans come to Hawai'i every year to walk in their idol's footsteps. A hotel on Kaua'i where he was "married" in one of his films afterward offered a popular honeymoon package and operated a small museum. Another, larger museum that included one of Elvis's cars was operated during the 1980s in Waikīkī by Jimmy Velvet, himself a popular singer during the 1950s. There's a professionally executed "Elvis in Hawaii" Web site at www.elvisinhawaii.com, operated by a fan in the Netherlands. Elvis memorabilia are sold in Waikīkī's International Marketplace, and some Elvis collectibles associated with Hawai'i have claimed unbelievable prices at auction. Reyn Spooner, the popular Hawai'i aloha-wear maker, markets a line of Elvis Presley clothing, some prints featuring album covers. Elvis Presley impersonators have been a staple in Waikīkī entertainment for more than thirty years. The longest-running Elvis fan club is based in Honolulu, the effort of a Hawai'i resident.

Without question, Elvis Presley, son of a sharecropper from Mississippi, whose Graceland mansion in Memphis, Tennessee, is the second most visited home in the United States (behind the White House), may be the single personality most closely identified with Hawai'i excepting those who were born and raised here. The décor of Graceland's "Jungle Room" reportedly was inspired by Hawai'i.

What follows is a journey into the past of "the last Hawaiian king," telling the story of Elvis's love affair with Hawai'i, and Hawai'i's love affair with the King of Rock and Roll.

Many unpublished photographs and other memorabilia are from long-lost or forgotten archives and from personal collections of memorabilia collectors and Hawai'i residents and fans.

Opposite, Tom Moffatt interviews Elvis at Honolulu Airport as he arrives wearing the yachting cap he'll wear in *Paradise, Hawaiian Style,* 1962.

CHAPTER 1

A New Hawaiian Kingdom

Hawai'i had many kings in its long and storied past, the last of them King Kalākaua, who reigned in the late 1800s. Elvis arrived more than half a century later, the unchallenged King of Rock and Roll. It seemed hard to believe that less than two years earlier he'd been a truck driver and roadhouse singer in Memphis, recording his songs for a small local company called Sun. After his contract was sold to RCA and "Heartbreak Hotel" was released in January 1956, the hits after that never stopped ("Hound Dog," "Don't Be Cruel," "All Shook Up," "Teddy Bear," etc.), and there seemed also to be no halting Elvis. By the time he arrived in Hawai'i, in 1957, he'd starred in three films, *Loving You, Love Me Tender,* and *Jailhouse Rock,* the title songs of which all went to number one on not just America's but most of the world's pop music charts.

For a long time, it was believed that Elvis's two shows at the old Honolulu Stadium on King Street—a site now occupied by a park—resulted from a wager. The way the story was told, Elvis was scheduled to end a national concert tour in October 1957 with two shows at the Pan Pacific Auditorium in Los Angeles. Elvis's manager, Colonel Tom Parker, a blustery, roly-poly man fond of expensive cigars, string ties, and hyperbole, said he wanted his "boy" to finish with two performances in Hawai'i. The Australian promoter Lee Gordon said the place was too small and remote, and he doubted the islands had enough Elvis fans to fill a stadium once, forget about two times.

The Colonel believed otherwise. Only a little more than a year had passed since Elvis burst onto the national scene, but the Colonel knew that of the 400,000 Christmas cards Elvis received in 1956, some 21,000 were from Hawai'i—an astonishing number, given the territory's relatively small population of 600,000.

The way Tom Diskin, one of the Colonel's lieutenants, later told the tale, the Colonel suggested a roll of the dice. If Gordon won, the tour would close in Los Angeles. But if he lost, Honolulu would be added, giving the Colonel's boy a chance for an island vacation following the two performances. (Performers appearing in Honolulu to this day make it the last stop of a tour for the same reason.) The Colonel won the bet. Years later, the Colonel said it wasn't true, leaving everyone to assume it was just another of the Colonel's good stories.

That wasn't the whole truth, either. The truth was that Colonel Thomas A. Parker was a fraud. His real name was Andreas (Dries) Cornelis van Kuijk, and he was Dutch, born in Breda, the Netherlands, in 1909, the son of a liveryman. As a teenager, he worked his way to America aboard a ship, returned to Holland for a visit, then went back to the United States, settling for a time in Atlanta, Georgia, where in 1929, although he was not an American citizen, he enlisted in the army under the name Andre van Kuijk and soon was sent to Hawai'i.

He was stationed first at Fort DeRussy and then at Fort Shafter, part of an antiaircraft unit of the Coast Artillery. His commanding officer

21,000 Isle Christmas Cards in '56 Gave Elvis Idea to Sing Here Sunday

Elvis Presley's manager, Colonel Tom Parker, said today the biggest incentive for the rock 'n roll singer's appearance here were the 21,000 Christmas cards received from Hawaiian Island fans last year.

The gyrating P̲r̲e̲s̲l̲e̲y̲ ... led to ... p.m., ... ched and ... back ... phis, ... on't ... out ... irs-

day" and two days later he was here making arrangements.

Original plans for an Australian tour were canceled, "but we may change our minds at the last minute," he said.

Presley, who grosses $800,000 annually, will be assisted on stage by the Blue Moon Boys, a band combo; the Jordannaires quartet, and a variety troupe.

Parker, who has been managing the money-making Presley for more than two years, describes his charge as "a very popular kid—but real humble."

According to Lee Gordon, show promoter, Presley is getting a guarantee on the show, "but I can't tell how much. It's in the contract."

Colonel Parker

at Shafter was named Thomas R. Parker, and when Andre wrote to his family in Holland, "Thomas Parker" was the name he used to sign his infrequent letters, advancing a secret campaign to replace his European origins with a new American identity. ("Colonel" was an honorary title given him years later by the governor of Tennessee.)

In time, Tom Parker stopped writing letters to Holland, severing all ties with his family, and after leaving the service, he settled in Florida, where he began his career as a promoter of circus and sideshow acts and then represented touring country music performers, helping promote their local appearances. In a few years, he shifted his base to Madison, Tennessee, a short distance from Nashville, where after managing Hank Snow and Eddie Arnold, he took a fledgling Elvis under his protective wing. Apparently he never told Elvis, or anyone else, about his Dutch past, but remembered his time in the islands fondly. So when the chance for Elvis to appear in Hawai'i came up, he grabbed it.

Because Elvis had promised his mother that he wouldn't fly more often than he had to, and time was planned between his Los Angeles and Honolulu shows, the singer traveled the 2,500 miles as many did in those pre–jumbo jet days, by boat. Moving everywhere with an entourage of good ol' boys from Memphis—eventually to be called, facetiously, the Memphis Mafia—he booked several state-rooms aboard the S.S. *Matsonia* and settled in for the leisurely four-and-a-half-day cruise.

On the *Matsonia* he met Kailua resident Velma Fisher, whose husband, Luther, was a Matson chief engineer. Velma and her four children occupied a cabin three doors away from Elvis's, and they met the first afternoon at sea when the singer and his entourage of friends came to the daily shipboard bingo game. Velma handed out the game cards and

Bottom, Elvis and other passengers arrive in Hawai'i aboard the *Matsonia,* 1957.

Jana, *left,* and Luana Fisher, *right*, pose with their "babysitter" en route to Hawai'i, 1957.

introduced herself. Elvis was twenty-five, she was forty-three, her son, Skip, was eleven, and her daughters, Jana, Luana, and Mona, were four, six, and nine.

"I didn't want to make a big fuss over him," Fisher remembers, "so I didn't ask for an autograph, but I did take pictures of him with two of the kids."

Elvis posed with the girls—his arms wrapped around their waists—wearing a loud, short-sleeved shirt, unbuttoned and knotted at the waist, sunglasses, and a Harley-Davidson cap, looking much like Marlon Brando in the motorcycle classic *The Wild One*, released three years before.

"He was always polite, a real gentleman," Fisher says, "and friendly. Every day at cocktail time in the lounge, he played the piano for everybody and he was real easy to meet. My daughters took to him, and I didn't mind leaving them in his care. He wasn't really a baby-sitter, but when I was away from the cabin, he looked in on them."

Fisher's nine-year-old, Mona, today remembers sitting on the piano bench next to Elvis. "He started singing 'Love Me Tender,' " she said. "He told me he wrote that for me! I believed that one for years."

Velma Fisher also remembers a young woman on the ship who said she had to

Top, Elvis with Mona Fisher, *at Elvis's right*, and three unidentified passengers; *bottom*, Elvis poses with another *Matsonia* passenger.

Elvis Sends Aloha

```
KHK165 RN MATSONIA WHEX 1 46 ANSTORP S 2015GMT

PRESSE HONOLULU STARBULLETIN HONOLULU

ALOHA VERY ENJOYABLE TRIP SUNBATHING SWIMMING TENNIS READING I KNOW I

WILL ENJOY YOUR ISLANDS LIKE TO SURF AND SWIM GETTING GOOD TAN ON BOARD

HAVE READ ABOUT HAWAIIAN HOSPITALITY AND AM EAGERLY LOOKING FORWARD TO

SAME BEST OF LUCK

                ELVIS PRESLEY
```

Teen-Agers Will See but Not Touch Elvis

Officialdom said today that Elvis Presley's fans will get to see him but not touch him when he arrives on the Matsonia at Pier 10 at 9 a.m. tomorrow.

He will come in on the ship, all right, officials said, but their plans are such that they predict no fan will get within 10 feet of him at the pier and few will get within yards of him at the Hawaiian Village Hotel where he will have a 14th floor refuge.

Security plans for Elvis match those for visiting chiefs of state.

A web of about 30 men, including personal guards, police officers, and Castle & Cooke security officers will surround the dock area.

Assistant Chief of Police Dewey Mookini said 22 additional men will be on call should there be any mob action.

Castle & Cooke is also ready with an extra guard crew—just in case things get out of hand.

Terminal officials reported a double fence may also be put up as an additional safeguard.

They said security measures mapped fo. the Presley entrance will make it

impossible for fans to get closer than 10 feet from the rock 'n' roll idol.

Chief Mookini believes that this reinforced security was never accorded any other person arriving here.

"Even (ex-President) Truman had about 20 men," he recalled.

But dockside preparations appear niggardly compared to the security strategy outlined at the Hawaiian Village Hotel, where the singer will be quartered in a 14th floor penthouse.

About a dozen men, including Al Pinoli, chief of security at the hotel,

Turn to Page 1-B, Column 3

Top, Elvis telegrams his fans via the *Star-Bulletin* on his way to Hawai'i, 1957; *bottom,* Elvis poses for a snapshot aboard the *Matsonia.*

meet Elvis. Velma took her to his cabin and knocked. The door opened. Elvis pulled the girl inside. The door closed. (Velma later said that when the ship arrived in Hawai'i the young woman came up to her in tears. Elvis had rejected her.)

Another incident caused Elvis and his friends worry. It was announced on the ship's public address system that a plane had gone down in the ocean nearby, so their arrival in Honolulu would be delayed while they joined the search.

"Elvis panicked," Velma recalls. "He said, 'My band is on that plane!' Well, it turns out they weren't, because they'd missed the flight.

We found out on our ship-to-shore radio that the plane had left Los Angeles without them because they were late getting to the airport."

There wasn't much for Elvis and his side-kicks to do on the long journey. This was before cruise liners became floating entertainment palaces. The idea of traveling by boat to the islands may have seemed interesting at first, but for this gang of fun-loving young men, four-and-a-half days at sea may have seemed at least three days too many.

The arrival in Hawai'i was less serene, with a crowd of several thousand fans gathered at the downtown Honolulu dock. Eddie Sherman and Bob Krauss, representing the *Honolulu Advertiser*, the morning newspaper, remember how difficult it was to hear Elvis's answers to their questions over the din. Pandemonium further greeted his escape from the ship, as his friends formed a football V-formation to get Elvis through the mob and into a fleet of limousines that took them to the Hawaiian Village Hotel.

In 1957, the Hawaiian Village's first tower,

Honolulu Advertiser columnist Eddie Sherman, *left*, and reporter Bob Krauss, *back to camera*, greet Elvis at the Aloha Tower Pier, 1957.

visit the fabulous

HAWAIIAN VILLAGE HOTEL

on Waikiki's finest beach

Bottom, Velma Fisher joins Elvis on Waikīkī Beach in front of his hotel.

at fourteen stories in height, was the tallest building in Waikīkī. Elvis and his buddies, his quartet of backup singers, the Jordanaires, and the four members of his band—who caught another flight to Hawai'i and arrived ahead of him—took the entire top floor. The Colonel was there, too, of course, having arrived a day in advance to be sure that all was ready.

In 1957, Hawai'i was far different from what it is today. This was where World War II began, with the Japanese attack on Pearl Harbor in 1941, and for the next four years it was the jumping-off point for more than a million U.S. fighting men engaged in the Pacific campaign. With the postwar downsizing of the military, agriculture became the primary "industry." Even so, tourism was growing—although the real boom was yet to come.

Not for another two years would Hawai'i become America's fiftieth state. Its population was greater than several states' in 1957, but unlike all the rest, a majority of Hawai'i residents were nonwhite, a factor that created strong opposition to statehood from many congressmen and senators from the southern states. In 1957, the people of the islands couldn't cast ballots in presidential elections; their governor was appointed by the U.S. president, and their single representative to the House of Representatives, another appointee, was voteless. America's best-known "Hawaiians"—excepting Duke Kahanamoku, the surfing and swimming giant who was an Olympic medal winner in 1912, 1920, 1924, and 1932—probably were the two members of the Kingston Trio who had attended Punahou School.

It was into this sleepy backwater that Elvis and his band of rockabilly musicians and gospel shouters arrived on November 9, 1957,

Tom Moffatt records a quick interview with Elvis for his radio show.

ready to kick off their blue suede shoes and put on the sexiest show since a line of hula dancers welcomed Captain Cook in 1778 and then seduced his crew.

It was on this visit that two disc jockeys, Tom Moffatt and Ron Jacobs, entered Elvis's life, or, rather, he entered theirs. Moffatt was a native of Detroit who worked as a junior staff announcer at KGU while attending classes at the University of Hawai'i in the early 1950s. While serving most of his military duty as a disc jockey playing records for patients at Tripler Hospital, he moonlighted at KGU as

an announcer and at KIKI, where he now says he played the first rock-and-roll record on the radio in Hawai'i, Bill Haley's "Rock Around the Clock."

Jacobs was born in Honolulu and after attending both Punahou and Roosevelt High School—failing to graduate from either—he began his radio career as a backup announcer at the Roller Derby. He was spinning records at KGU when, in 1957, Henry J. Kaiser started a radio station atop the Hawaiian Village Hotel, thus its call letters KHVH. At the time, Kaiser was in his seventies and as a developer was soon to change not only the sound but also the face of Honolulu, building Hawai'i Kai and Kaiser Hospital. One of the first things he did was hire Jacobs and Moffatt, who along with Honolulu's senior radio veteran, who called himself J. Akuhead Pupule, moved into the rooftop studios in the newly constructed hotel.

A day before Elvis's concert, Moffatt and Jacobs hatched a plot to have an Elvis look-alike "tour" O'ahu in a convertible. The station's engineer, Donn Tyler, would wear an Elvis wig and sit in the back of the car along with someone dressed to resemble the Colonel, while Jacobs drove around the island, stopping from time to time to use a pay phone to call Moffatt, who was on the air and playing only Elvis records.

Colonel Parker, with his ever-present cigar.

The stunt was enormously successful, and when Jacobs and Tyler returned to the studios, Moffatt had to play several Elvis records in a row to hide their laughter. That's when Tyler, still in his Elvis garb, stepped out onto the balcony to look down on the crowd of fans below.

"We didn't know it," Jacobs wrote years later in HONOLULU® Magazine, "but Elvis had been floating scarves, records, and shreds of Hawaiian Village linen down to the mob. When Tyler appeared, the screams tripled in volume. He stood wiggling and waving, milking the moment. Then he reached up, lifted off the top of his head and tossed the greasy black wig to the faithful below. A thousand screams turned to dazed silence."

That was when the Colonel called from his room directly beneath the station rooftop studio, saying he wanted to see them. Fearing the worst—Jacobs said he had visions of the French Revolution—they hurried down one floor and were led past a guard and into the Colonel's suite. The Colonel was seated next to the phone, wearing a string tie and a straw hat and holding a thick cigar.

" 'You boys got a pretty fair sense of humor,' he said. 'Now, I heard your little stunt. And you know what? It should sell some tickets.' "

Jacobs said he felt as if someone had untied the blindfolds and sent the firing squad home.

" 'Suddenly, Elvis himself appeared,' Moffatt recalled. 'I remember how quiet, almost bashful, polite and warm he was.' "

Jacobs described the Colonel's introduction. " 'Elvis, say hello to Mr. Moffatt.' They shook hands. Elvis said, 'Pleased to meet you, sir. Sure is a pretty place y'all got here.' Then I was introduced. Unflinching eye contact, firm handshake, high voltage electricity. 'Good to meet you, sir,' softly said the owner of the voice singing 'Blueberry Hill' on the radio. He called me 'sir,' I thought. He's two years older than me."

The Colonel then suggested that Moffatt and Jacobs emcee the concert the next day. Elvis said, "Yes, sir!" and left.

Rain threatened the following day, but the skies cleared, and after an opening performance by Sterling Mossman, a local comedian, and some songs by Elvis's band,

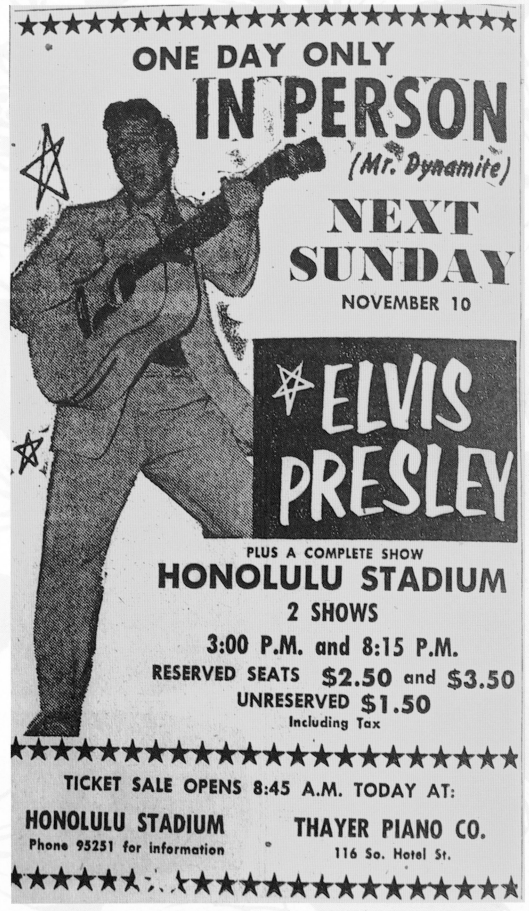

Newspaper advertisement for Honolulu Stadium shows; note ticket price.

Well, maybe he'll learn to like the music when he grows up. Honolulu Stadium, 1957.

Hawai'i's most successful show promoter, bringing the Rolling Stones and many more headliners to the islands, it was the most exciting performance of his career.

"The sound and lights were nothing to compare to today's standards," Moffatt recalled. "The sound system was pretty much what they used for boxing, and the lights were the ring lights overhead, but that didn't matter with the raw excitement projected by Elvis Presley.

"One thing I will never forget was his encore number. He had just done 'Hound Dog,' started to go off the stage, and of course the crowd went crazy. So, he came back and he did this slow, sexy version of 'Hound Dog.' He jumped off the stage and sang to the audience. And the barriers were nothing like they are today, just a piece of fencing. So you could see Elvis through the fencing, and he was down on his knees singing. Then he was swept away in a limo with his band, another car following closely behind containing the Memphis Mafia."

At a press conference the next day at the hotel, Moffatt interviewed Elvis and asked him how he liked the nonstop Elvis music he'd played the day before.

"Well, I enjoyed it for a while," he said, "but after a while it got boring to me, so I changed the station."

Elvis spent his final evening in Hawai'i on the beach in front of the hotel, signing autographs.

an intermission was called. That's when the Colonel and E.K. Fernandez, a Hawai'i promoter known for bringing carnivals and circuses to the islands, moved into the audience to sell photographs.

"Take whatever bill they hold up," the Colonel told Fernandez, "and don't give nobody no change."

The two shows were unremarkable and, simultaneously, the most remarkable events of the season. As was true for so many of Elvis's performances, it was nearly impossible to hear anything for the screams. So for the audience all was lost, musically. Yet to Moffatt, who later went on to become

There's no question how she feels!

He's neither the first nor likely the last, but Jonathan Von Brana is Waikīkī's longest-running Elvis impersonator, billing himself as an "Elvis impressionist."

The World's First Elvis Impersonator

"We would never be able to get to Elvis," Ron Jacobs later said in HONOLULU® Magazine, "but we could create our own Elvis. I blurted out the plan to (Tom) Moffatt. 'Elvis sails in tomorrow, limousines to the hotel, goes to his room, and doesn't come out 'til show time Sunday. After Elvis is in the hotel, we bring out the imposter. Then we do a play-by-play on the radio, me taking The King on a tour of Oʻahu."

Who would play Elvis? Moffatt was too well known from his TV dance show and emcee work around town, and Jacobs was dis-

qualified by his red goatee. They settled on Donn Tyler, the station's production manager. He was younger and smaller than Elvis, but with the help of a makeup artist from the Honolulu Community Theatre, who "fashioned a hairpiece with enough grease to lube a Harley Davidson" (quoting Jacobs again), the phony Elvis was prepared. Another friend, Ray Freed, was given a pillow to stuff under an oversized coat, a guitar to carry, a straw hat, and a fat cigar.

As Elvis unpacked his three suitcases in Room 14-A, Jacobs and Tyler and Freed climbed into Jacobs's two-tone Ford Skyliner, its retractable hardtop folded away in the trunk. "A handful of fans spotted us climb into it," Jacobs wrote. "We heard our first screams of the day. Tyler must have looked authentic. Besides, the kids had heard about it on their portable radios, so it had to be true."

Moffatt kept the scam going: "Elvis is out there somewhere on Oʻahu and you'll hear about it only on KHVH. He might pull into your driveway and ask, 'Have I Told You Lately That I Love You?'"

First stop: the girls' dorm at the University of Hawaiʻi, where Jacobs cranked up the car radio— Moffatt was playing "I Got a Woman" by now—and the three-story building emptied from the top and a horde of girls

Bruno Hernandez, just three years old in 1990; at the time, his dad, Pete Hernandez, leader and manager of the Love Notes, a popular Waikīkī musical group, called him "the world's youngest Elvis impersonator."

rushed the car. Tyler consented to give one autograph, and "as [a girl] wailed like an air-raid siren," Jacobs recalled, "I stomped on the gas and took off." Now Tyler was laughing hardest. He said he'd signed his real name.

After making another quick phone call, the merry pranksters drove through the Pali Tunnel, which had opened just six months before, as Moffatt announced, " 'Attention, Windward Side! Elvis is visiting your neighborhood!' " In Kailua, Jacobs began station-hopping on the radio to see if anyone else had picked up on their hoax, and when he got to KGU he heard pregame announcements for a football game between McKinley and Punahou high schools. That decided the next

destination: the stadium where Elvis would appear the next day.

The car's top was lowered again as the trio fast-talked their way past a guard at the gate and drove onto the stadium track. The KGU announcer, Gene Good, saw the car as the phony Elvis stood up. Stopping in the middle of a sentence about one of the teams, he then "raved hysterically. 'Ladies and gentlemen, believe it or not, Elvis Presley, the King of Rock 'n' Roll, has pulled into Honolulu Stadium!' " Jacobs slowly circled the field, chased by half the McKinley band, as the Punahou band struck up "Hound Dog." And Gene Good continued to babble.

"So tidy two minutes ago, now the field was strewn with tubas, helmets, buckets, yard markers, buff-and-blue and black-and-yellow pompoms, footballs, bass drums, confetti, and ushers wandering in circles," Jacobs wrote. "Tyler urged we leave now—before being surrounded, overwhelmed, exposed, and left hanging from the goal post."

Enough, they decided, was enough, and they raised the car's top a final time and returned to the hotel without further incident.

"The 'Elvis Hoax' is what the Colonel wanted to call it," Moffatt said years later, when he and Jacobs reminisced with the Colonel. "Ron wanted to call it the 'First Elvis Impersonator,' and the Colonel didn't like the word 'impersonator,' because he said, 'No one could impersonate Elvis.' "

CHAPTER 2

Elvis Remembers Pearl Harbor

In the following two years, Elvis's life traversed tumultuous twists and turns. Soon after his 1957 concerts in Honolulu, he was ordered to report to his draft board in Memphis and not long after that he was inducted into the U.S. Army, showing himself to be a superpatriot, declining offers to perform for the military's enlistment program, preferring, he said, to serve like any other draftee. While he was in training at Fort Hood, Texas, his mother died, and later, while serving with a tank company in West Germany—and rising to the rank of sergeant—he met Priscilla Beaulieu, a U.S. Air Force officer's young daughter, then sixteen, who'd later become his wife.

In August 1959, when Elvis was still in Germany and more than a year from his discharge date, the Colonel was vacationing in Hawai'i and decided to do some test marketing. He met with disc jockey Ron Jacobs, who along with Tom Moffatt had left KHVH and now was anchoring Hawai'i's top rock station, KPOI, and gave him a large roll of blank paper from a teletype machine. The Colonel said that if KPOI could get enough signatures to fill the roll, he would see that it was

delivered to Elvis in Germany and the first concert he performed when he returned to the States would be in the islands.

To back up the stunt—carried out at the newly opened Ala Moana Shopping Center, where KPOI employees and their friends staffed a table to collect signatures—Moffatt interviewed Elvis on the telephone, the only interview Elvis gave during his two-year-long army service.

While Moffatt was on the air, hosting his popular *Uncle Tom's Cabin* program, he called Elvis, catching the young sergeant while he was on duty, so the conversation was limited in time. As always, Elvis's answers were brief. No, he didn't have any special girlfriend and in his spare time he usually answered fan mail and yes, he'd probably let his crew cut grow out when he left the army. In closing, when Moffatt asked if he had a message of aloha to his Hawai'i fans, Elvis said, "Well, I would like to say that I will never forget the day the ship pulled out, what a good feeling I had. It was a wonderful feeling I will never forget. It, ah, when I left Hawai'i, everybody was throwing the leis in the water, you know? And everybody was singing 'Aloha' and all

Opposite, Elvis arrives in Honolulu for the *Arizona* Memorial benefit concert.

Top, Colonel Parker delivers a telegram from Elvis to Tom Moffatt, *left,* and Ron Jacobs, *right,* in the KPOI studios, 1959; *bottom,* the telegram.

that. It was really a nice feeling and I certainly hope to come back again someday, I really do."

About the same time, Elvis sent a telegram to the Colonel, then staying at the Hawaiian Village Hotel, saying, "My sincere thanks to Tom Moffatt and Ron Jacobs and the entire staff of KPOI and to all the fans and friends in the Hawaiian Islands. I am in full agreement with you that if [at] all possible we should make our first personal appearance after I return from the army in Hawaii. Perhaps you can work this in with our first tour after we make our first movie next year. Your pal Elvis Presley, 14 Goethestr, Badnauheim, Germany."

Simultaneously, in Hawai'i, a campaign aimed at building a memorial to the men who died during the Japanese attack on Pearl Harbor on December 7, 1941, was floundering. The monument was to be erected on the site of the U.S.S. *Arizona,* where 1,102 officers and men remained entombed in the sunken battleship beneath harbor waters. An estimated $500,000 was needed, in all, and only about half had been raised, an insufficient sum to start construction.

George Chaplin, the editor of the *Honolulu Advertiser,* a veteran of World War II who served on the staff of the *Stars and Stripes,* the wartime daily, wrote an article asking for more public support and sent it to newspapers all over the United States in advance of what was then the nineteenth anniversary of the Japanese attack. Chaplin wanted construction to begin in time for the twentieth anniversary and said only $50,000 was needed to make a difference.

When the Colonel saw Chaplin's plea reprinted in the *Los Angeles Herald-Examiner,* he called the *Honolulu Advertiser* and reportedly said, "I know a young man whose services can be a big help." He also said that if Chaplin arranged an appropriate venue and paid for the tickets, ushers, lights, sound system, security, and all the rest of the technical and personnel costs, Elvis would donate his services (at that time generally valued at $25,000 for a concert), along with those of his backup singers and band, and at least one supporting name act. Chaplin and the Pacific War Memorial Commission, headed by H. Tucker Gratz, happily agreed.

Thus, the concert that the Colonel talked about for Honolulu when Elvis left the army became a certainty, and a charity event at that. It would not be his first performance following his discharge, however. That would be held in Memphis, a benefit for the Elvis Presley Youth Center, which was to be constructed on land behind his birthplace in Tupelo, Mississippi.

Colonel Parker, *left,* gives an autographed photo to H. Tucker Gratz, *right,* chairman of the War Memorial Commission, 1961.

While holidaying in Hawai'i in 1965, Elvis talks at Pearl Harbor with H. Tucker Gratz, War Memorial Commission chairman, and Rear Admiral Henry S. Persons, Commander of the Pearl Harbor Naval Base.

Not wishing the *Arizona* benefit concert to cost him anything, the Colonel went to NBC, asking the network for $50,000 in return for rights to film the concert as part of an Elvis special. In this fashion, the Pacific War Memorial Commission would receive enough money to hold a dedication ceremony and begin construction within a year, and the Colonel would recoup the cost of flying everyone to the islands and paying the performers. Ownership of the program would revert to Elvis after a single broadcast, and at the same time, Elvis would gain public stature as a man who supported good causes, especially one so patriotic and uncontroversial.

As it turned out, plans for the TV show collapsed. Instead, in January 1961, the Colonel returned to Hawai'i three months ahead of the benefit show to hold a press conference, announcing that after the performance, Elvis would remain in the islands to make a movie. In this way, Paramount Pictures would cover many of the expenses.

Radio promotion for the concert in the 4,000-seat Bloch Arena on the U.S. Navy base was low-key compared with the circus in 1957. The Colonel bought half an hour on all thirteen O'ahu radio stations, playing selections from Elvis's first religious album, *His Hand in Mine,* on the first anniversary of Elvis's mother's death. Jacobs produced and Moffatt narrated. The outsized white cardboard tickets, each measuring 2 ¹/₄ by 4 ¹/₈ inches, with a picture of Elvis printed on it, were sold for a top price of five dollars. This was double the price charged at the Honolulu Stadium four years earlier—except for three hundred that were set aside at a cost of one hundred dollars apiece, many of them for seats to be occupied by senior officers.

"Naturally all the generals and admirals came to the Colonel, trying to get to Elvis," Jacobs remembered. "And so the Colonel started snowing them about how important they were to the security of the world and how patriotic and so on, and if they'd line up, why he'd give them a little something from Elvis. So they lined up, all these guys in charge of the Pacific and parts west, and Parker went over to a trunk and carefully, almost secretly, pulled some tiny color pictures out and very stingily doled them out, one to each admiral and general. Later, he showed me the inside of the trunk. It was full of eleven-by-fourteens in color, eight-by-tens in color, calendars, record catalogs, you name it. He told me he thought all the brass deserved was little pocket calendars.

"Then one of the admirals came to him, asking for complimentary tickets, and the Colonel said no—even if Presley's father came

The Colonel behind him, Elvis arrives in Hawai'i, greeted by a "Hawaiian chief"; see page 83 for a Pan American brochure autographed on the flight.

to the benefit, he'd have to pay his way in, why even Elvis bought his ticket. Then the Colonel made sure the Negro chauffeur he'd been assigned was given two free tickets right up front next to all the brass."

Minnie Pearl, the country comedian whose husband Henry Cannon had piloted a plane for Elvis early in his career, was booked as Elvis's opening act and was on the plane with Elvis. "They held us on the plane until everybody got off," she said. "There were twenty-five hundred screaming women at the airport. Jimmy Stewart [who was on the same flight] got off and they didn't even recognize him. They were pushed up against the fence. Elvis went along, shaking their hands. They lined the streets all the way to the hotel. They'd shout, 'Ellllvvviiissssss!'

"Tom Parker, who was with us, said to stay with Elvis," she recalled years later. "He wanted me in the pictures. We pulled up at the Hawaiian Village Hotel, which has a sort of lanai out front—the lobby isn't enclosed. There were five-hundred women there and as we got out of the taxi, Elvis grabbed my arm and the women broke and mobbed us.

"I felt my feet going out from under me. My husband was behind me, trying to get to me, and he was screaming, 'Get out . . . get out!' I just knew I was gonna be killed. I

Top to bottom: Minnie Pearl, wearing her trademark hat, at the Grand Ole Opry in Nashville; Elvis signing an autograph; Sterling Mossman.

never felt so close to death. You know, everyone wants to be Number One, but that one experience was enough to convince me I don't want it."

A press conference was held later in the day—attended not only by the local media but also by nearly a hundred student reporters from all of O'ahu's high schools and middle schools—and the concert followed at Pearl Harbor that night. There were two opening acts. Minnie Pearl was on the bill because the Colonel remained loyal to the country performers who gave him his start, and for the military men in the audience who were from the American South. The other was Sterling Mossman, the same local comic he'd used in 1957. They were greeted warmly, but neither was the entertainer anyone came to see. Then Elvis's band performed several instrumental numbers.

In all, the audience waited an hour and a half, and then, during the intermission, watched the Colonel move through the military attendees and fans with *Honolulu Advertiser* columnist Eddie Sherman selling "Elvis pitchas" for whatever the two could get, repeating his routine of 1957 at the Honolulu Stadium.

"The Colonel grabbed a bunch of eight-by-tens," Sherman recalled, "and he says to me, 'I'll sell 'em, you collect the money, and whatever they give you, one dollar, five dollars, ten dollars, don't give 'em any change.' "

Finally, it was time for the King. Wearing a gold lamé jacket with silver-sequined lapels and cuffs, and thumping on a guitar inlaid with mother-of-pearl, Elvis delivered a performance that the local newspapers called, quaintly, a "crackerjack show" and a "boffo extravaganza." Afterwards, many of the adults told reporters they couldn't hear much because of all the screaming, but

This photo of Elvis trying to disengage himself from a clinging fan appeared on the front page of the *Honolulu Advertiser* the morning after the concert.

1. HEART BREAK HOTEL
2. ALL SHOOK UP
3. FOOL SUCH AS I
4. I GOT A WOMAN
5. LOVE ME ———— INTRODUCE THE BAND
6. SUCH A Night
7. RECONSIDER BABY
8. I NEED YOUR LOVE tonight
9. That's ALL Right
10. ~~DOING the Best I CAN~~
     DON'T BE CRUEL
11. ONE Night
12. ARE YOU LONESOME tonight
13. NOW OR NEVER
14. SWING DOWN
15. Hound Dog

Gary
These are the songs
we did in show
E. P.

Following his Pearl Harbor show, Elvis wrote out the song sequence and sent it to Gary Pepper, a wheelchair-bound fan in Memphis.

glowing praise came from Peter Guralnick in his biography *Careless Love: The Unmaking of Elvis Presley*. "Even with the very poorest home recorder–quality sound," he wrote, "you have only to listen to the tape of the performance that has survived to sense the energy that was coming off the stage, to get a whiff of the ferocity of feeling that the music unleashed. . . . [T]here is a sheer joyousness, a guttural exuberance of expression that refuses to be denied.

"By now the band had been playing together off and on for just over four weeks and Elvis eggs them on with an enthusiasm not just for what they are able to do, but for what they are able to permit him to do. Again and again he urges guitarist Hank Garland to solo, indicating his appreciation with grunts and exclamations that have nothing to do with the audience. The music crests and surges with an impulse all its own, and Elvis calls for Hank to solo again, he demands another sax solo from Boots [Randolph], he forgets the words, even loses the structure of the song, but embraces the moment with pure, uninhibited feeling. To Boots it was 'one of the highlights' of his life, and to Jordanaire Gordon Stoker, who had worked with Elvis steadily since 1956, there was a spontaneity to his performance that most closely resembled a man being let out of jail."

Gordon Stoker recalled that at one point Elvis fell to his knees and slid twenty feet to the front of the stage with the microphone in his hands, never missing a note. "We thought he was going right off the edge," he said. "Ray Walker [the quartet's bass voice] was so surprised, he didn't come in harmonically where he

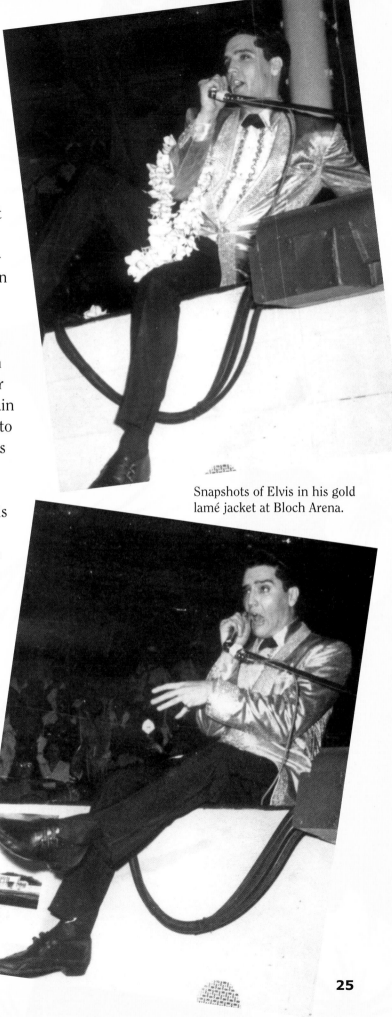

Snapshots of Elvis in his gold lamé jacket at Bloch Arena.

Playing air piano—or massaging a musical note?

With funding having successfully been raised, the construction of the U.S.S. *Arizona* Memorial was well under way in March 1962.

was supposed to. He just stood there with his mouth open, and nothing was coming out."

Elvis sang nineteen songs, his longest show ever. Ticket sales totaled $47,000, to which Elvis and the Colonel added another $5,000, pushing the benefit over the top.

Two weeks later, a letter to Vernon Presley dated April 8, 1961, from Herman Lum, the Clerk of the Hawai'i House of Representatives, accompanied House Resolution 105, expressing "gratitude and appreciation to Elvis Presley and Colonel Tom Parker on behalf of all Hawaii for their services in helping to raise the funds needed for the U.S.S. *Arizona* Memorial."

Elvis's concert also was credited with helping revive national public sentiment for the Memorial. That September, Congress was prodded into donating $150,000, and then the Hawai'i legislature added $50,000 to a previous contribution of the same amount. With $250,000 more in federal and state funds and $275,000 in public contributions, the Memorial was completed.

The concert was a fitting close to a stage of Elvis's career. It would be eight years before he sang in public again.

Hawai'i's Number One Elvis Fan

Charlie Ross is a dedicated woman. A Hawai'i resident best known as founder and president of the Elvis Memorial Fan Club Hawaii, she came to the islands in 1978 to escape the cold winters in her native Chicago, flying one year and a day following Elvis's death because she didn't want to travel on the anniversary.

It was after settling into an apartment in Honolulu and starting a local fan club that she started banging on U.S. Parks Department doors, trying to get someone, anyone, to do something about giving Elvis the sort of recognition she thought he deserved for help- ing fund construction of the *Arizona* Memorial. And she's still banging today.

"The navy and the parks people say they don't want his name out there on the Memorial, they only want the names of the war dead, and I can go along with that," Charlie says. "But I don't think it's too much to ask to have a little wooden plaque at the landing, or a bench or something. Surely they must know that without Elvis, there would be no *Arizona* Memorial."

After discovering there were no fan organ- izations in Hawai'i, she founded the club, a branch of an organization called the Elvis Worldwide Memorial Fan Club, and when that club folded soon afterwards, she decided to continue as an autonomous club, hence the new name. In 1980, when the National Park Service assumed management of the U.S.S. *Arizona* Memorial from the navy, she says, "We suddenly found ourselves with a cause célèbre."

Up to that time, Charlie recalls, there was a large proclamation standing on the Memorial naming all those, including Elvis, who had contributed to the building of the Memorial. There was also a smaller plaque, given to Elvis and the Colonel from the navy. But when management of the popular visitor attraction changed hands, the proclamation and plaque were removed.

"For years, we asked fans to write to the Park Service, and they did," Charlie says. "The Park Service developed a form letter with a lot of half-truths, including the lie that Elvis did not want recognition. Nonsense! Elvis vis- ited the Memorial on a number of occasions in the 1960s and never requested anonymity. When we wrote to legislators, they just deferred to the Park Service again. So much for that effort! We even wrote to the President, who claimed to be an Elvis fan, but none of our letters ever reached his desk."

Petitions were circulated, but they were ignored as well. It's been more than forty years since Elvis's benefit concert pushed the drive to raise funds for the Memorial over the top and allowed construction to begin. And it's been more than twenty years since Charlie first launched her own campaign. So far, she's had no success, but she hasn't stopped her letter writing, and she continues to push for recognition by encouraging other fan support through her quarterly newsletter.

Over the years, other fan clubs exploited the Hawai'i connection, such as the Blue Hawaiians E.P.F.C., edited in Beverly Hills in the 1970s, but Charlie is still president of the only fan club in Hawai'i and one of the few currently recognized by the Elvis Presley Estate. Those interested in joining, or who want more information, may write to her at P.O. Box 11295, Honolulu, HI 96828, or send an e-mail message to elmemh@earthlink.net.

ELVIS ALOHA FROM HAWAII
ELVIS MEMORIAL FAN CLUB HAWAII
Post Office Box 11295
Honolulu, Hawaii, 96828
Charlie Ross, President
and newsletter editor
elmemh@earthlink.net

January, Februar

Top left, club newsletter; *bottom right,*
Charlie Ross, president of the Elvis
Memorial Fan Club Hawaii since 1978.

CHAPTER 3

Blue Hawaii

Just as there were such easily identified formula films as "the Jerry Lewis movie" and, before that, "the Abbott and Costello movie" and "the Bing Crosby/Bob Hope road movie," and the Busby Berkeley musical, and movies celebrating the Hardy Boys and the Three Stooges and the Marx Brothers, in the 1960s there was something called "the Elvis Presley movie."

Even by the time *Blue Hawaii* was made in 1961, Elvis's films were so individualized, they were a category unto themselves, most appearing to be little more than an excuse to get Elvis into a recording studio to produce

another soundtrack album. Such recordings would comprise most of his prolific outpouring of song until he opened in Las Vegas in 1969, and because he often cranked out three and sometimes four films a year, frequently the music was as weak as the cinema.

This was not entirely true for *Blue Hawaii*. For this film and soundtrack LP, recorded in Los Angeles before Elvis went to Hawai'i for the *Arizona* benefit, fourteen songs were cut in just three days, an unusual accomplishment by later standards, when some rock bands took months, even years, to produce an album. The material included some of the filler associated with his earlier,

Two stills from *Blue Hawaii*; *right*, with Joan Blackman.

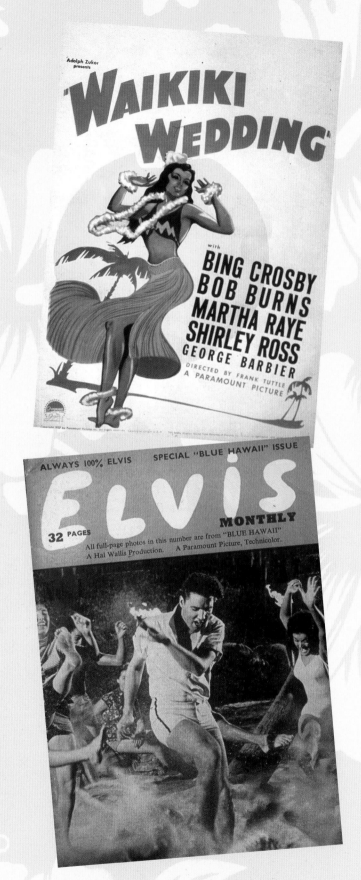

and later, movies—songs written on order by men who never really understood Elvis or rock and roll, such as "Rock-a-Hula Baby," "Beach Boy Blues," and "Ito Eats."

But the selection also included some good material, notably the movie's title song, "Blue Hawaii," previously recorded by Bing Crosby in 1937 in another Paramount motion picture, *Waikiki Wedding*, and noted, justifiably, for its refrain, which delivers Hawai'i's quintessential promise: "Dreams come true/In blue Hawai'i." In addition, there were two of the most popular compositions from Hawai'i's large and estimable songbook.

One was "Aloha 'Oe," a poignant musical farewell and one of the best known of all Hawaiian melodies, written by Hawai'i's last queen, Lili'uokalani, and inspired, she said, by a trip by horseback she made to a friend's ranch in Maunawili in 1878. By the time Elvis recorded it, the song had become a staple in every Hawaiian vocalist's repertoire and was used to close countless island performances, including those of the Royal Hawaiian Band, playing at the Honolulu docks for departing cruise liners.

The second was "Ke Kali Nei Au," better known as "The Hawaiian Wedding Song," included in an operetta staged in Honolulu in 1925 by Charles E. King, one of the most revered and prolific of Hawaiian composers. Always performed as a duet between lovers, it climaxed Elvis's *Blue Hawaii*, just as it did a nightly dinner show at the Coco Palms Hotel on Kaua'i, where many of the film's scenes were shot.

Finally, there was "Can't Help Falling in Love," a song based on an eighteenth-century French melody. This appeared on the B side of the single timed for the film's release later in the year—the A side was a much weaker Twist number, "Rock-a-Hula Baby," inserted at the last minute to capitalize on the current dance fad—and it became Elvis's dramatic, and obligatory, show-closer when he performed in concert in Las Vegas and on the road in the final years of his career.

The four songs, as a set piece, or even taken separately, resonated with the sensuality and longing identified with the islands and, sadly, would be equaled rarely in future Elvis films.

The picture itself was constructed professionally. It was produced by Hal Wallis, who served in the same role for three of Elvis's previous seven films, *Loving You, King Creole,* and *G.I. Blues,* and later would produce another four. It was directed by another veteran of the Hollywood studio system, Norman Taurog, who directed *G.I. Blues* the previous year and would go on to direct another four of Elvis's movies. The screenwriter, Hal Kanter, had written or directed films for Bob Hope, Rowan and Martin, Pat Boone, and Dean Martin and Jerry Lewis. Over the years, Kanter worked numerous times with Hal Wallis—for whom he adapted Tennessee Williams's *The Rose Tattoo*—and had directed *Loving You,* Elvis's first movie for Wallis. This provided Elvis with the comfort that can accompany familiarity—assuming the relationships were stress free, and in

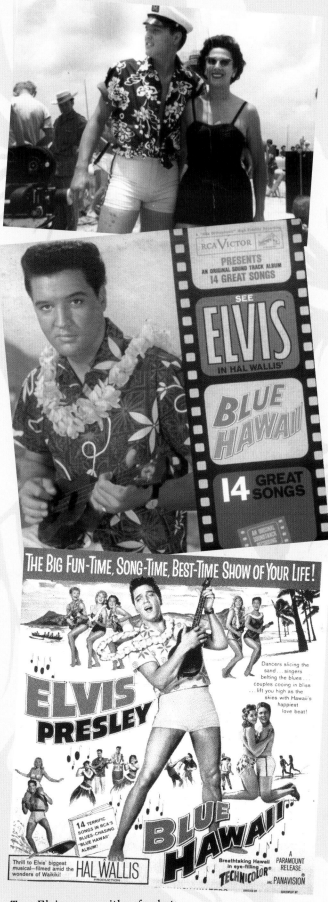

Top, Elvis poses with a fan between scenes.

ELVIS PRESLEY
BLUE HAWAII

HAL WALLIS PRODUCTION · CO-STARRING JOAN BLACKMAN · ANGELA LANSBURY · NANCY WALTERS · DIRECTED BY NORMAN TAUROG · SCREENPLAY BY HAL KANTER · A PARAMOUNT RELEASE · TECHNICOLOR AND PANAVISION

this case, they were—and gave the film's location shooting the sort of effortlessness that goes with working together and knowing what works and doesn't work.

Elvis also took to the island environment if not like a native, at least like a man who enjoyed beautiful Polynesian women, the soft tropical climate, the scenery, and Hawai'i's relaxed way of life. In the film, he genuinely appeared to be enjoying himself.

Equally important, Elvis may have been lip-synching to the prerecorded songs, but only good vocalists can make this common deception seem so facile and convincing.

As was already customary in Elvis's film-making, seasoned or well-regarded actors were given supporting roles, for the same reason that weak singers used practiced backup singers and other recording artists used studio

musicians rather than the members of their actual bands: to make the lead performer sound and look better. Thus, *Blue Hawaii*'s cast included Angela Lansbury (after seven months on Broadway in *A Taste of Honey*), who played Elvis's scatterbrained mother, although she was only thirty-five to Elvis's twenty-six at the time. Other roles were played by Roland Winters, a character actor whose credits then ranged from *Abbott and Costello Meet the Killer Boris Karloff* to 1960s *Cash McCall,* and John Archer, who had a well-established reputation playing leads in B pictures and supporting roles in A pictures. The noted island performer Hilo Hattie also appeared briefly in one scene.

Blue Hawaii's original title was *Hawaiian Beach Boy.* The film was based on a story by Allan Weiss, a former Los Angeles newspaper

34

Elvis on Round Top for a scene in *Blue Hawaii,* 1961.

Top to bottom, scenes from *Blue Hawaii*: a not-so-warm welcome at Honolulu Airport; one of many memorable song numbers; Angela Lansbury and Roland Winters as Elvis's parents.

reporter. In it, Elvis plays Chad Gates, returning to the islands after two years in the army, determined not to join his father's pineapple business. Instead, he takes a job with a tourist agency, where his half-French, half-Hawaiian girlfriend, Maile, played by Joan Blackman, works. The scenes that follow conveniently allow Elvis to sing, first at a welcome-home party (Chad's mom doesn't like Maile, his father does), then at various locations visited while escorting a teacher and four schoolgirls around O'ahu. This tour concludes at a luau, where Elvis gets into a fight and goes to jail. His father bails him out, but he is fired by the tourist agency, and when his parents blame Maile for the incident, he leaves home. Fortunately, the schoolteacher hires him to resume the tour, and they travel to Kaua'i. There are predictable romantic misunderstandings, but in the end all is resolved. Chad decides to open his own agency with Maile and convinces his father's boss to use the agency to plan its next convention. The movie ends with a colorful boat-ceremony wedding (filmed at the old Coco Palms Hotel in Kaua'i) that even mama approves.

This simplistic recitation of the plot line ignores the movie's beauty and charm. Elvis was Elvis, after all, and most of the music and all of the settings could not be faulted. In fact, the outstanding performances of *Blue Hawaii* may have been those played by Hawai'i's luscious scenery—including Waikīkī Beach, the Ala Wai Yacht Harbor, Punchbowl, Ala Moana Park, Hanauma Bay, Tantalus, and the Waioli Tea Room on O'ahu; Anahola, Lydgate Park, and the Wailua River on Kaua'i. It almost seemed as if someone had been told to bring Hawai'i's best postcards to life.

In many ways, the location "shoot" had the character of a holiday. Elvis had his boys with him, and Charlie O'Curran, Hal Wallis's longtime choreographer, who also worked with Elvis on earlier films, brought his wife, the singer Patti Page, leading to numerous evenings of music around the hotel piano.

Still, it was the Colonel who stole the show sometimes. When shooting moved to Hanauma Bay, Ron Jacobs recalled, "There had to be fifty-seven technicians and directors and script girls and makeup men and all the rest standing around with reflectors, waiting for the clouds to clear so the light would be just right for a matching shot. Finally, the sun comes out and they have twenty-six seconds to shoot. Elvis is ready. Everybody is ready. The director calls 'Action' and Parker comes out of the bushes, on camera, screaming for Hal Wallis. Wallis comes rushing up. The shot's been blown. He's furious, but he's trying to keep control, even if his face is purple. He asks Parker what's wrong and Parker says Elvis is wearing his own gold watch in the shot and the contract doesn't call for his providing wardrobe, but that's okay, so long as they come up with an additional $25,000 for the use of the watch." Elvis removed his watch and shooting resumed.

Elvis apparently wasn't having so much fun. Minnie Pearl said she and her husband stayed at the Hawaiian Village for a week following the Pearl Harbor concert, into the first days of the film's production, and "the whole time we were there, Elvis never got out of his room except to work. They say he came down in the middle of the night to swim. He couldn't come down during the day. He had the penthouse suite on top of that thing there and we'd get out and act crazy, having the best time in the world, and we'd look up there and Elvis would be standing at the window, looking down at us."

Blue Hawaii was released in time for the

Top to bottom: Elvis with his *Blue Hawaii* girlfriend, Maile (Joan Blackman); playing a tour guide on Kaua'i; in a fight; and with his screen dad, played by Roland Winters, *left,* and his boss, played by John Archer.

Thanksgiving-Christmas holidays, and when it completed its run in approximately five-hundred theaters in the United States in early 1962, it had grossed $4.7 million, a minuscule sum by today's standards, but ahead of most of the pack at the time, achieving the number eighteen spot on *Variety*'s annual list of box office champs in the year of its release, and number fourteen the following year.

In addition, the soundtrack album became the fastest-selling LP of 1961 and occupied the top position on all album sales charts for much of 1962, eventually racking up more than $5 million in sales—also a huge sum for the period—and outselling all of Elvis's studio albums.

While the film also helped put Hawai'i on the map worldwide—giving many of the state's numerous beautiful settings glorious technicolor exposure—its financial success made it an easy guess that Elvis would be coming back for more.

In the long history of movies made in Hawai'i, *Blue Hawaii* remains one of the true classics. Forty years later, it frequently appears on television and in 2001 was used by the City of Honolulu to open an every-weekend program of films shown on a big screen erected on Waikīkī Beach.

CHAPTER 4

Girls! Girls! Girls!

A year later, with the sweet smell of the success of *Blue Hawaii* still as fresh, and alluring, as that of Hawai'i's aromatic *pīkake*, ginger, and plumeria, Elvis returned to the islands with many from the earlier crew. Hal Wallis was producer again and Norman Taurog was behind the camera calling "Action!" and "Cut!" but this time they produced an inconsequential piece of fluff with a title that seemed (as many of Elvis's titles did) generated by a computer or a studio publicity hack: *Girls! Girls! Girls!*

It was a boom time for Hawai'i. With a new airport and jets arriving daily, tourism was accelerating and Waikīkī was going high-rise. Ground was broken for the East-West Center on the University of Hawai'i campus. And the U.S.S. *Arizona* Memorial, designed by Honolulu architect Alfred Preis, was dedicated, quickly becoming one of the state's prime visitor attractions, as was intended.

Elvis had made two more films since he'd been in the islands for *Blue Hawaii*, playing a hillbilly in *Follow That Dream* and a boxer in *Kid Galahad*. With his earnings going to $600,000 plus 50 percent of the profits for each, he became one of the highest-paid Hollywood stars. He'd moved into a new

Laurel Goodwin, *left,* and Stella Stevens, *right,* pose with Elvis for a publicity photo.

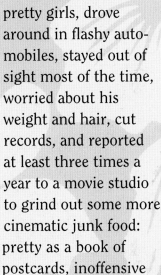

house in Bel Air, with expanded room for his buddies, all of whom had assigned responsibilities attached to their relationship with Elvis, but were also expected to provide companionship.

His lifestyle seemed as set as the movies' plots. He played football with his friends, rode motorcycles, dated pretty girls, drove around in flashy automobiles, stayed out of sight most of the time, worried about his weight and hair, cut records, and reported at least three times a year to a movie studio to grind out some more cinematic junk food: pretty as a book of postcards, inoffensive to a large demographic, and as foreseeable as the school holidays when they were released. From 1961 until 1968—the date of the videotaping of his first television special, which marked the beginning of his public return—Elvis starred in twenty-one films, an average of three a year, and the release dates usually coincided with spring break and summer and Christmas school holidays.

For *Girls! Girls! Girls!* again Elvis arrived in the islands by air, traveling the last distance from the airport to the Hawaiian Village Hotel by helicopter, where he was met by the usual throng and heaped with flower leis until only his nose was showing, making him look

Opposite, Elvis displays his bedroom eyes in *Girls! Girls! Girls!*

much like the winner of the Kentucky Derby. Atop his head, he wore a navy blue peaked sailor's cap that was to be a part of his wardrobe through most of the movie. He was interviewed on his arrival by Tom Moffatt, still a disc jockey for KPOI.

Again, there was plenty of music to get Elvis—who played a sometime shrimp boat, sometime charter boat captain—from scene to scene. It may be considered unkind to say that shrimp fishing has never been a big thing in Hawai'i, but that was how the script read, and the tunesmiths-for-hire followed right along, thus "Song of the Shrimp" and "We're Coming in Loaded."

Of the thirteen cuts on the soundtrack album marketed with the film—just in time for year-end holiday moviegoers in 1962, repeating the release schedule for *Blue Hawaii*—only one deserved praise. This was "Return to Sender," written by Otis Blackwell, a rhythm-and-blues singer who composed "Fever" (a hit for Little Willie John in 1956, winning greater success two years later as a torch song for Peggy Lee) and, for Elvis, two of his biggest singles from the same period, "Don't Be Cruel" and "All Shook Up." But even "Return to Sender," the letter returned serving as a metaphor for failed love, was in the novelty-ballad vein, absent the muscle that had characterized the music of both Blackwell and Elvis in their early collaborations.

Even the title song, written by Jerry Leiber and Mike Stoller, composers of maybe more great rock-and-roll songs (including most of the early Coasters' hits and "Hound Dog" and "Jailhouse Rock") than any other songwriting team, failed to find an audience.

In the film, Elvis plays Ross Carpenter, a skipper of a charter fishing boat, who works for a man who also owns a sleek sailboat built

Top to bottom, scenes from *Girls! Girls! Girls!:* Elvis as charter fishing boat skipper Ross Carpenter; dancing and sailing with actress Laurel Goodwin.

13 of The Coolest Songs in RCA'S Fabulous "Girls! Girls! Girls!" Album!

Copyright © 1960 by Hal B. Wallis and Joseph H. Hazen. A Paramount Release. Printed in U.S.A.

Bottom, in Mexico, *Girls! Girls! Girls!* underwent a title change.

by Ross's father just before his death. A local nightclub singer, Robin Grantner, played by Stella Stevens, is in love with Ross, but it is to another woman, Laurel, played by Laurel Goodwin, that he is drawn, telling her of his desire to own the boat one day. Suddenly the dream is dashed when the owner is forced to sell the craft to a broker, portrayed by Jeremy Slate, who offers its resale at double the price. Elvis goes to work on one of the broker's tuna boats and takes a second job singing in the club where Robin works.

Secretly, Laurel buys the sailboat for him, but Ross feels humiliated by the charity and departs for Paradise Cove to stay with friends. Laurel follows with the boat broker at the wheel. Ross storms aboard and punches the man, but that night back at the cove, he realizes his error and asks Laurel to marry him.

It's worth mentioning that the script was credited to Edward Anhalt, a versatile scenarist who would, two years later, win an Oscar for scripting *Becket* and later write *Jeremiah Johnson* and *The Right Stuff,* among many other distinguished films. One may reasonably assume that his putting words in Elvis's mouth was not subsequently emphasized on his résumé and that his motivation for getting involved at all had something to do with money. That, or he turned over all his writing duties to his credited cowriter, Allan Weiss, who remained friendly with Wallis following the success of *Blue Hawaii* (based on his novel).

Considering the title, the picture had, oddly, only two girls in it, at least in prominent speaking roles: Stella Stevens and Laurel Goodwin, who with Elvis formed the perfect and predictable triangle, with Jeremy Slate looming as a villain (of sorts; there are seldom any serious threats in Elvis Presley movies). Benson Fong was cast as Elvis's Chinese sidekick, and they even conversed in Chinese (again, of sorts).

It might be mentioned that the lead love interest, Miss Stevens, a former *Playboy* centerfold, before taking this role opposite Elvis played Appassionata von Climax in the film version of *L'il Abner*. Although she and Elvis seemed to have a lot in common, at least geographically—she was born only a year after Elvis in Coffee, Mississippi, and had attended Memphis State University—years later in an interview she said they didn't get along. She offered no details.

As for Elvis, his performance had sunk along with the quality of the material. The plot was so flimsy and the musical material so lame, he appeared to be walking through the scenes in his sleep.

Neither the film nor the soundtrack album fared as well as *Blue Hawaii*, but Paramount and RCA were not particularly disappointed. The picture quickly slipped into the profit column. The LP rose to number three on U.S. charts and was certified gold, and the title song rose to the top of the singles list.

Hawai'i didn't suffer any, either. In the background, again it looked like paradise, and Elvis was still the Hawai'i Visitors Bureau's best friend, its favorite unofficial ambassador. Significantly, though, the film's setting is never specified and could be anywhere from Louisiana to the West Coast.

The yacht he wants and the girls he's got.

Karate and the Kalihi Connection

Elvis met Ed Parker in 1960, when Parker was giving a lecture-demonstration of *kenpo* karate to a group of doctors in the Beverly Hills Hotel. Despite his *haole* name, he was part-Hawaiian, a native of Kalihi, the "local" neighborhood adjacent to downtown Honolulu, a graduate of Kamehameha Schools, with a degree in sociology and psychology from Brigham Young University in Provo, Utah, where he began teaching professionally. He opened his first karate studio in Pasadena, California, in 1956 and within a few years became a popular exponent of his chosen martial art. Elvis was twenty-five when he approached Parker, then twenty-nine, saying he wanted to learn more about the body contact sport that he'd begun studying while in the army.

Elvis strikes a karate pose on his NBC special.

"He felt like I was kind of a rebel in my field, as he was in his," Parker later wrote for an English fan magazine. "I didn't accept a lot of the Oriental methods, because I knew they didn't work on the street, but a lot of the other aspects could be revamped so they would be applicable.

"His mother meant an awful lot to him, and he talked about how she kept him from physical activity for fear he might get injured or hurt. Now that she was gone, he found karate to be an avenue of pursuit that he wanted to be involved in, because he wanted the activity and the knowledge that stemmed from it. He talked to me about the fact that he was different than others. He was basically a very shy guy."

It was not until 1968, when Elvis was vacationing in Hawai'i with his wife, that he encountered Parker again, at a karate championship at the Honolulu International Center. It was also then that they both met a twenty-five-year-old former champion named Mike Stone, another part-Hawaiian, who later would play a key role in the Presleys' divorce.

Elvis incorporated karate moves and poses in his "comeback" show on NBC-TV that same year, and in 1969, as Elvis prepared to return to the concert stage in Las Vegas, Parker offered to train him to work even more karate into his act, as well as to better prepare himself should the need for self-defense arise. Parker said that's when their friendship began, and he became a regular visitor back-

Left, karate moves on a California stage, 1970.

People Report — Honolulu Advertiser — Wednesday, September 7, 1977

Parker: "To be honest with you, he was just like a local guy: Loyal, considerate, natural and extremely generous."

Ed Parker

Elvis' bodyguard

stage and in Elvis's Vegas suite, serving as one of his onstage bodyguards in 1970 when Elvis received some death threats. In time, Elvis included full demonstrations of karate in his performances, with Parker sitting contentedly in the audience.

The relationship continued, on and off, with Parker awarding Elvis a sixth-degree black belt in 1973, not because Elvis was so skilled, but because such awards sometimes were given to celebrities to help advance the sport and, in this instance, Parker's own career. That same year, Parker put Elvis's name on a marquee, in San Francisco, failing to get his permission. Angry, Elvis sent some of his guys to get his name off the marquee, and it was several months before he and Parker talked again.

By the end of the year, all was forgiven and, encouraged by the success of a television series starring David Carradine called *Kung Fu* and the posthumous release of Bruce Lee's *Enter the Dragon,* Elvis and Parker began talking about making a film of their own. Against the Colonel's wishes, Elvis gave Parker some start-up money.

The film never happened, probably because the Colonel never approved and Elvis got distracted. But Elvis and Parker remained friends, with Parker arranging some of Elvis's activities during one of his vacations in Hawaiʻi. He also wrote a deferential memoir, *Elvis and Me,* published in 1978, a year after his former student's death. Parker died in 1990.

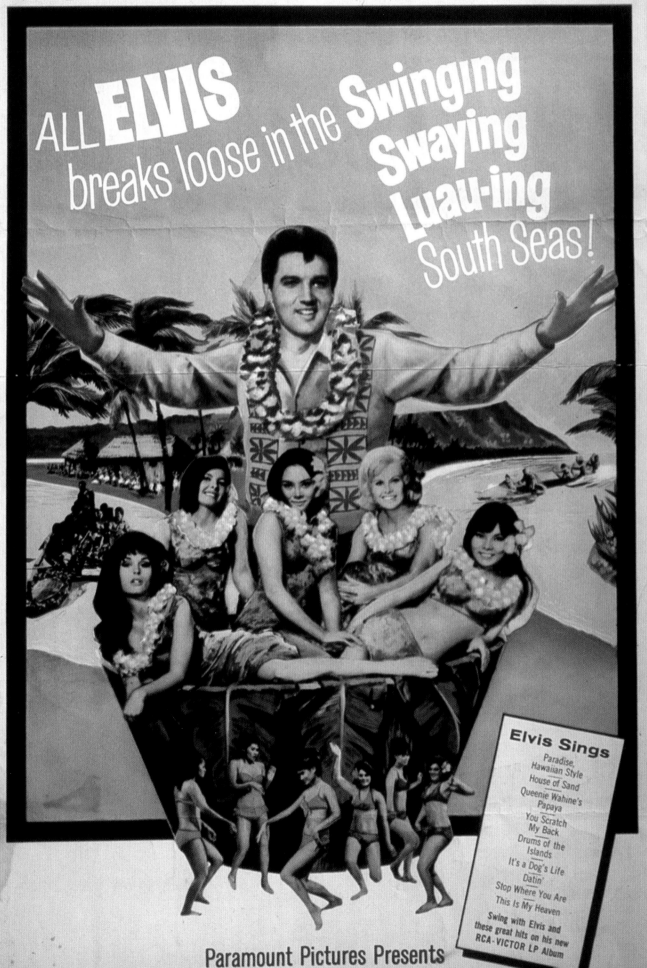

CHAPTER 5

Paradise, Hawaiian Style

In 1966, four years after the release of *Girls! Girls! Girls!,* Elvis returned to Hawai'i for his third and final island film.

Hawai'i had changed since his last visit. Tourism continued to grow, as did the population, and 1966 was the year that satellite live television transmission from the mainland was inaugurated, but the most noticeable difference was that, just as was the case during World War II, the islands again became a primary military staging area and R&R destination, for America's war in Vietnam.

For Elvis, the changes were big, as well, and not all of them were positive. In 1962, he was the reigning king of the pop music world, yet in just one year his crown was knocked askew and in danger of falling off. The challenges came from all sides: from the Beach Boys in California and the so-called "surfing sound"; from Bob Dylan and electric folk music and the accompanying sounds of political and social protest; and, most significantly, from England, where the rhythm and blues that so influenced Elvis years before now was put through a different filter by the Beatles and the Who and the Rolling Stones. John Lennon may later have said that "before Elvis, there was nothing," but it was Elvis's beachhead that Lennon and his cohorts stormed.

By 1966, the United States was torn apart by civil rights marches and sit-ins, demonstrations opposing the war in Vietnam, and open rebellion that championed long hair on men and psychedelic drugs and free sex for all. One of the popular lapel buttons of the time read, "Make Love, Not War." John Kennedy had been assassinated. Nothing was the same after that.

What was Elvis doing? He was making movies called *Roustabout* and *Girl Happy* and *Harum Scarum* and *Tickle Me.* In one, *Double Trouble,* in which he was in love with two women (thus the title), he sang an updated version of "Old MacDonald's Farm." As one of his costars put it, "The philosophy seemed to be, don't say it if you can sing it."

He was rich now, earning as much as $750,000 for each film (plus 50 percent of the profits), and he had that big house in Bel Air along with Graceland, but there were people now saying, so what?—people who thought he was passé, irrelevant, a cultural antique headed for the dustbin of history. In 1966, Elvis was thirty, and according to Abbie Hoffman and a large part of the youthful population, that was too old to trust.

However archaic Elvis may have seemed to some, the Colonel believed that when you had a successful formula, you didn't tinker

Top, scenes from *Paradise, Hawaiian Style,* 1966; *opposite,* Elvis with his *Paradise, Hawaiian Style* girl-friends, actress Suzanna Leigh behind Elvis.

with it. So it was no surprise when the Colonel said he and Elvis were going back to Hawai'i with Hal Wallis. For this film, a long-time Wallis assistant, Michael (Mickey) Moore, who worked with Elvis in *G.I. Blues* and *Blue Hawaii,* made his directorial debut, and the script, based on his own story, was written by Allan Weiss, along with Anthony Lawrence. Years later, Weiss said, "Wallis kept the screenplays shallow. I was asked to create a believable framework for twelve songs and lots of girls."

In *Blue Hawaii,* Elvis's character worked on the ground, escorting tourists around the islands in cars, on horseback, and on foot. In his second island film, *Girls! Girls! Girls!,* he was a charter boat captain, sharing with his fans a vision of Hawai'i by sea. Now, in a movie originally titled *Polynesian Paradise,* Wallis had Elvis's character taking to the tropical air.

Of the three pictures, this one, ultimately titled *Paradise, Hawaiian Style,* has the thinnest, and most preposterous plot, wherein Elvis is a pilot named Rick Richards who sug-gests a partnership in a helicopter tour com-pany with an old friend, another pilot, Danny Kohana, played by James Shigeta (a native of O'ahu, then establishing his name in Hollywood). Danny is reluctant, but gives in when Rick says he'll get his many girlfriends who work at hotels to provide customers, which they agree to do. However, Rick is rejected by the new company's Girl Friday, played by Suzanna Leigh.

Rick gets into immediate trouble while transporting a load of unruly dogs and nearly hits a car driven by a Federal Aviation Agency official, who grounds Rick and threatens to cancel his license if he flies again. Things get worse when Rick takes Danny's nine-year-old daughter, Jan, played by Donna Butterworth,

Top, Elvis with some of the Polynesian Cultural Center performers.

for a ride in the helicopter and she hides—
and then can't find—the ignition key. When
Danny locates Rick and Jan the next day, he
tells Rick their partnership is over and then
heads for home in his own helicopter, crash-
ing en route. Rick mounts a successful rescue
mission and tells the FAA that he flew only to
save his friend. He's allowed to continue flying, he and Danny are friends again, and Girl
Friday decides that she likes Rick after all.

As the loopy story was filmed, a few com-
parative high spots came when Wallis took his
crew to the Polynesian Cultural Center, a
popular tourist attraction on Oʻahu's windward side, operated by the Church of Latter
Day Saints. Here, in Lāʻie, were a Mormon
temple and Brigham Young University, whose
students—many from all over the Pacific—
worked part-time in the center to earn tuition
credit, serving meals, demonstrating traditional island crafts, and wearing costumes in

On the movie set at the Polynesian Cultural Center.

highly commercialized but generally authentic pageants of song and dance, several of which were incorporated into the script. This gave Elvis a larger musical canvas than he'd had in his previous island films, where generally he broke into song (and fistfights) on beaches and in small nightclub settings.

As usual, the female love interest was little more than scenic. Miss Leigh was a shapely blonde who started appearing in pictures, most of them lightweight, at fifteen—she was now twenty-one. Before *Paradise, Hawaiian Style* came *The Pleasure Girls* and *Boeing Boeing,* the latter a Jerry Lewis comedy, and later, *The Deadly Bees* and *Lust for a Vampire.*

On the plus side was Hawai'i's own nine-year-old Donna Butterworth, who starred opposite Jerry Lewis the previous year in *The Family Jewels* and who nearly stole several scenes in this film, too, as Jimmy Shigeta's daughter; she sang two songs with Elvis, one of which, "Sand Castle," was cut from the film but included in the soundtrack album. Years later, she was one of many youthful island singers and composers to appear on a series of "Homegrown" albums sponsored by a local radio station (and produced by Ron Jacobs). But not even an adorable child could save the movie's torpid story line.

The music was anemic, too, forcing Elvis, once again, to sing novelty songs, the best—

or worst—example likely being the one called "Queenie Wahine's Papaya," inspired, perhaps, by one of the ditties that were so numerous in Hawai'i during the 1930s and 1940s, "Princess Poopooly Has Plenty Papaya." Such music had a long and successful history in the islands, although much of it was composed by Caucasians—*haole*s, as the Hawaiians call them—as was true in the 1960s when writers in New York and Los Angeles were commissioned to write for what came to be regarded as Elvis's latest beach picture.

Elvis included similar melodies in all of his filmed-in-Hawai'i movies, to middling approval. Much of the criticism came because the music seemed diluted, the lyrics sappy and trivial, compared with the depth of emotion and force displayed in his earlier rock (and religious) performances. But the genre was legitimate, however shallow, and in that context, a critic should only ask: were the songs in *Paradise, Hawaiian Style* worthy? Unfortunately, they were not, and not even the Colonel could find one he wanted to release as a single.

Perhaps this was one reason that the Colonel tried to get the Beatles to sing a song with Elvis at the film's conclusion. The Beatles' film contract with United Artists precluded any such notion, however, and the only time Elvis met the Fab Four, it was at Elvis's Bel Air estate, where Ringo Starr

Playing a ukulele for some *keiki o ka 'āina,* Donna Butterworth in center.

played pool with some of Elvis's buddies, George Harrison smoked a joint and talked about Hinduism with Elvis's hairdresser (who had given Elvis a number of spiritual books), John Lennon and Paul McCartney eventually picked up a couple of guitars and jammed a little with Elvis, and the Colonel and Brian Epstein gambled at a coffee table that turned into a roulette wheel.

At the same time, the most convincing romance associated with the film occurred behind the cameras, where one of Elvis's side-kicks, Jerry Schilling, fell in love with an island girl, Sandy Kawelo, a student at Brigham Young University and an employee at the Polynesian Cultural Center. The best fights erupted off-camera when the film's director used a Samoan war canoe in the production number for "Drums of the Islands,"

which was based on a Tongan chant. Tongan paddlers were used for the scene as well, and the Samoans took offense.

Elvis's fans hadn't all fallen victim to the English invasion, and however lacking the plot and music and other ingredients key to determining the critical success of a film, *Paradise, Hawaiian Style* survived the test of the theaters and music stores. That said, this success was even less than that which greeted his earlier island films, and it was to be Elvis's final "beach picture."

Paramount released *Paradise* in May 1966, for the out-of-school summer audience, and the $2.5 million earned at the box office pushed it only to number forty in the list of the year's top-grossing films. The soundtrack album peaked in *Billboard* magazine at number fourteen.

Canoeing at the Polynesian Cultural Center, before the fists started flying.

James Shigeta

James Shigeta, shown here with Elvis in *Paradise, Hawaiian Style,* was once America's foremost Asian-American film and television star.

James Shigeta was thirty-three years old, just two years older than Elvis, when he made *Paradise, Hawaiian Style.* For a time, Shigeta was the biggest Asian-American star, but America's interest in films with Asian themes gave him, over time, an up-and-down career.

The *nisei*—Hawai'i-born, second-generation Japanese—son of a Honolulu contractor, he majored in English at New York University, aspiring to be a teacher and writer, enjoying singing as a hobby. An appearance on television's *The Ted Mack Original Amateur Hour* led him to a singing career, which in turn took him to Las Vegas, where he was persuaded to take a lead role in *Walk Like a Dragon,* produced by Paramount and novelist James Clavell.

In 1961 he hit it big as the lead in Ross Hunter's version of the Rodgers and Hammerstein musical *Flower Drum Song,* starring with Nancy Kwan, herself a rising star following her lead opposite William Holden in *The World of Suzie Wong.* That's also the year he portrayed, in a fact-based romantic drama, *Bridge to the Sun,* a Japanese diplomat married to a Tennesseean (Carroll Baker) when events at Pearl Harbor forced them to leave America.

By the time he appeared with Elvis, the interest in Asian themes and stars had waned, and Shigeta played out most of the rest of his career in supporting roles in films and on TV.

How Hawaiian Was He?

Much criticism has been heaped on Elvis, the Colonel, and others who controlled his creative (or not so creative) output, especially during the Hollywood years. The question most often asked was: how true were the pictures to what Elvis had to offer, and could become? The answer frequently was: not at all. Many considered—and still regard—Elvis's acting career largely wasted, however eagerly his fans greeted most of the cardboard roles.

Similarly, it's fair to ask: how faithful was Elvis to Hawai'i in his three island movies? Surely he was a big fan of the islands, and the scenery never looked better, nor was it displayed any more widely by others, not by the hundred or so other films made in Hawai'i over the years, or in the most popular television series produced in the islands, *Hawaii Five-O,* with Jack Lord, and some years later, *Magnum, P.I.,* with Tom Selleck.

And it wasn't just the scenery. The "feeling" was often Hawaiian, too, and so were the story lines (however flimsy) and costumes. Sometimes you heard some Hawaiian words, in dialogue as well as in the songs (although it must be added that when bongo drums and a

tambourine came out on a beach in *Blue Hawaii*, and Elvis pronounced Kaua'i as if it were spelled "cow-eye," most Hawai'i residents rolled their own cow-eyes and fell into the theater aisles laughing).

In Hawaiian music, there is a genre called *hapa haole,* meaning "half-Hawaiian," the presumption being that there is a mixture of Hawaiian and Caucasian influences. The term is used to describe a song that has predominantly English lyrics interspersed with one or more Hawaiian words. The instrumentation likely is Hawaiian, but not exclusively, and the song's subject surely will be, but the tune's structure and "sound" are western.

When talking about Elvis, in the end it comes down to the music. Elvis may have been a movie star, even a cultural icon, but what he was first and last was a singer. And a vocalist is dependent to a significant degree on material—in fact, to a larger degree than some vocalists might admit. So when we ask how faithful Elvis was to Hawaiian music, we have to take a look at the composers of the original *hapa haole* music.

Many were Tin Pan Alley songwriters who cranked out material starting in 1915, when steel guitars and sensuous hula dancers from Hawai'i became staples on the vaudeville and music hall circuits in the United States and England. Thus songs such as "They're Wearing 'Em Higher in Hawaii" (the grass skirts—get it?), "O'Brien Is Tryin' to Learn to Talk Hawaiian," "When Those Sweet Hawaiian Babies Roll Their Eyes," and "Oh, How She Could Yacki Hacki Wicki Woo." Another song using gibberish as Hawaiian, "Yaaka Hula Hickey Dula," was a big hit for Al Jolson. Most of the composers of these songs resided in New York and had never been to Hawai'i.

Other composers were *haole* residents of the islands, including bandleader Harry Owens, composer of "Princess Poopooly Has Plenty Papaya"; another bandleader, Don McDiarmid, who gave singer-comedian Clara Inter her signature song, "Hilo Hattie Does the Hilo Hop"; R. Alex Anderson, who penned "Cockeyed Mayor of Kaunakakai"; and Johnny Noble, who wrote "My Little Grass Shack" and the English lyrics for "Hawaiian War Chant."

The songs composed for Elvis's movies may not have joined such classics as these, but there's no argument, he definitely sang *hapa haole* songs, at least technically, in what might reasonably be called *hapa haole* movies, a genre that probably has not, until now, been named.

CHAPTER 6

Aloha by Satellite

The Colonel was known for staging colossal events—or making small ones seem larger than they were—and the idea he announced in 1972 was one of his biggest and best, a concert to be broadcast worldwide by satellite from the Honolulu International Center Arena (since renamed the Neal Blaisdell Center) in January 1973.

The Colonel saw President Richard Nixon live by satellite from China and thought, if Nixon can do it, Elvis can, too. The show would begin after midnight, Hawai'i time, to allow the live performance to be viewed in prime time in Australia, New Zealand, Japan, Korea, Thailand, and the Philippines, and by American servicemen in Southeast Asia. The next night the show would be shown in twenty-eight European countries via a Eurovision simulcast. NBC-TV would air the concert in the United States. Ultimately, the Colonel said, Elvis would be seen by a half-billion people.

There'd been big changes for Elvis since he'd been in Hawai'i to make *Girls! Girls! Girls!* Most important, he became a father in 1968, with the birth of a daughter, Lisa Marie, and only four years later, Priscilla left him for the island-born karate teacher Mike Stone. About the same time, Elvis made his stunning "comeback" on an hour-long NBC television show and initiated a much praised and commercially successful series of appearances at

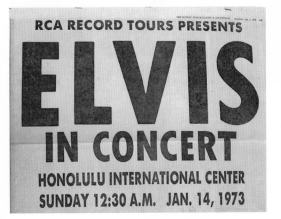

the Hilton Hotel in Las Vegas, and then triumphantly went back on the road again.

He also paid a surprise visit to Nixon in the White House, volunteering to help with his antidrug campaign in return for a federal narcotics badge for his growing collection of police enforcement medallions.

There were changes in Hawai'i, too. The war in Vietnam had become what local historian Gavan Daws described as "a running sore," with protests left and right, and uniformed men still transiting, although by now in smaller numbers. The economy was booming, driven mainly by real estate. Chris Hemmeter was working on a deal that would replace the Waikiki Biltmore with the state's first megahotel, the Hyatt Regency. Condominiums were sprouting like mushrooms. Tourism continued expanding to the outer islands. And on the entertainment scene a club called the Dunes featured lunches served by topless-bottomless waitresses and waiters.

The satellite show, to be called "Aloha from Hawaii," was announced on the final day of Elvis's month-long engagement in Las Vegas, September 4. Sitting next to Elvis was RCA's president, Rocco (Rocky) Laginestra, who helped Elvis and the Colonel make it clear that this concert not only would claim history's largest audience, but also would be

Opposite, a jowly Elvis at the press conference announcing the satellite show, 1972.

In 1961, the Hawaiian Village Hotel joined the Hilton chain.

"the first time in the history of the record industry" that an album would be released within days of the performance, an attempt to keep the inevitable bootlegged recordings at a minimum and capitalize on the widespread exposure.

It was only after that, with just four months to showtime in Hawai'i, that the Colonel and Bob Sarnoff, the president of the NBC-TV network, began serious talk about who would produce and direct such an effort. The individual suggested by Sarnoff was Marty Pasetta, a Californian then in his late forties whose forte was the entertainment special. An independent who didn't work for any network, he had a forceful personality and a proven ability to juggle many complicated details simultaneously, a claim backed up by his directing the Emmy, Grammy, and Oscar shows for television, as well as the Ice Capades. He also produced and directed Bing Crosby, Glen Campbell, and Perry Como specials and five Don Ho specials in Hawai'i, so he knew both music and the islands well.

"The way I got it," Pasetta said later,

"Elvis had liked the first NBC show, the one he did in 1968, but he wasn't knocked out by all the production. He wanted the pure sense of a concert. NBC called me and I went to look at Elvis in performance in Long Beach. I expected to see a gyrating person moving all over the stage. He was far from that. He was staged, quiet. In fact, I was wondering how I was going to make an hour-and-a-half show sustain without anybody else on it with what I saw. I went back to discuss it with NBC and they said, 'You're on your own—discuss it with the Colonel.' "

What Pasetta and others didn't, or wouldn't, acknowledge at the time was the reason for Elvis's sluggishness. Elvis's growing dependence on prescription drugs and his high-fat diet had outdistanced his love of karate and racquetball, and the King of Rock and Roll was, in a single, shocking word of description, fat. His face and torso were bloated, and he had lost much of the stamina that characterized earlier performances, resulting in shows that lasted less than an hour.

The tour was one of Elvis's easiest, with

Eddie Sherman introduces Elvis at a press conference to announce that the satellite show will be a benefit for the Kui Lee Cancer Fund.

short flights to Tucson, El Paso, and Oakland, and after that, leisurely drives from his Los Angeles home to the big auditoriums in nearby San Bernardino and Long Beach. Elvis and his troupe then took a full day to travel to Hawai'i and settle into—and throughout—the thirtieth floor of the Hawaiian Village Hotel, now managed by the Hilton chain.

The two Honolulu concerts were tacked onto the end of the tour, mainly, as always, for the cash. Elvis was still traveling with a pack of friends who made real his every wish. This lavish lifestyle, coupled with a generosity that provided cars and other expensive gifts and occasionally houses, made it necessary for the Colonel to keep his boy working as much as possible.

Shortly after the satellite show was announced, Eddie Sherman, still a columnist for the *Honolulu Advertiser,* noticed that no tickets would be sold to the concert—as was required by law for any production that was to be broadcast on the public airwaves—and that "contributions" would go to a then unnamed charity. Sherman had met Elvis on the *Matsonia* in 1957, and in 1961 was assigned by the *Advertiser* to stick close to the Colonel during the *Arizona* Memorial concert. Figuring he thus might have an "in" with the Colonel, he wrote a letter suggesting that the charity be the Kui Lee Cancer Fund, named for a beloved Hawai'i singer and composer who died at age thirty-four.

"My secretary didn't mail the letter," Sherman recalled years later. "But it didn't matter, because the next day, Matt Esposito, the manager of the Honolulu International Center, where the show was to be staged, invited me to have lunch with the Colonel. So I gave him the letter in person. The Colonel said it wasn't his call, it was up to RCA, because they were putting up the money. At the same time, he said in any case, he expected the *Advertiser* to promise full cooperation."

Elvis had recorded one of Kui Lee's songs, "I'll Remember You," on an album released in 1964, the year of Lee's death, and with everyone's approval it was agreed within a few days that contributions to both the dress rehearsal and televised show would go to the fund that was then being administered by Sherman.

The Honolulu concerts in 1972 were unremarkable. Elvis had lost some weight for

Kui Lee's widow, Nalani Lee Meadows, at the show with her three children and Eddie Sherman.

the tour now ending, but still remained out of shape. It didn't matter. The loyal island audiences, thrilled to have their king back on an island stage after more than a decade, didn't seem to notice, and when Elvis appeared with Kui Lee's widow, Nalani Lee Meadows, at the press conference that followed, the questions were so mild as to cause doubt about the reporters' credentials. In fact, many represented their high school newspapers—as was the Colonel's custom at previous Hawai'i press conferences—and the Colonel honored them all. He wanted puffballs pitched at his boy, and puffballs were what he got.

"What about marriage in the future?"

"Uh . . . I haven't thought about it. I have a little girl, four years old. It's hard to put the two, marriage and the career, together."

"Are you a religious person, Elvis?"

"It's played a major role in my life, gospel music. I like it. We often go into our suite and sing all night."

"How do you account for your success after seventeen years?"

Elvis laughed. "A lot of praying, sir."

Once again, Elvis had pulled it off, appearing somewhat jowly, but otherwise untouched by time, still the southern gentleman, still generous—he and the Colonel each wrote a personal check for $1,000 to the fund, as did Jack Lord—still boyishly innocent and ebullient.

After seeing Elvis in the Long Beach Arena,

Tom Moffatt greets Elvis at the airport on his arrival for the satellite show, the Colonel looking on.

Marty Pasetta took a few sketches of stage design to the Colonel and said he wanted to build some excitement into the show. "I wanted to put a ramp in, I wanted to lower the stage, I wanted to get closer to the fans and the people, I wanted to generate excitement, so they could get to him," Pasetta said. "And the Colonel said no, no, no to everything. Finally he said, 'Well, you take it up with Elvis.' I said, 'Okay, I'll take my shot and go.' "

Elvis was vacationing in Las Vegas in October when Pasetta first met him. When he went upstairs to Elvis's suite alone, Elvis was flanked by three of the singer's sidekicks. As the producer sat down, the three took out silver-plated pistols and laid them on the table. Pasetta was visibly shaken, but plunged ahead.

"I saw your show in Long Beach and I didn't think it was all that exciting," he said.

The three bodyguards sat forward in their

chairs, and Elvis just looked at Pasetta, his eyes hidden behind sunglasses.

"But," Pasetta continued, beginning to sweat, "I've got a lot of ideas about how to make it an exceptionally exciting television show."

Elvis was amused by the producer's brashness, and when Pasetta said he had to lose weight, he took off his glasses, threw back his head, and laughed. They spent the next four hours talking, and when Pasetta left, it was with Elvis's arm draped casually over his shoulder.

"Y'know," Elvis said, "this is the first time I've ever sat with a producer for longer than a half-hour. Normally, they come in and talk to me and they're out."

Elvis went home to Memphis after that and started "taking care of business," a phrase that was his motto and that was hanging around the necks of so many of his friends and associates—on gold pendants that carried the symbol of a lightning bolt and the letters TCB, which meant "Taking Care of Business," in a flash.

Elvis was genuinely excited by the satellite challenge, and once he was back behind the Graceland gates, he began to exercise and diet like a man possessed. He increased the frequency of his karate workouts and consumed large quantities of vitamins and protein drink. He also helped the process along with diet pills, losing twenty-five pounds in a month.

Quickly, the pieces came together. Usually a new costume was designed only for Las Vegas, but Elvis wanted something special for Hawai'i, so he asked Bill Belew to make an all-white outfit with a huge eagle on the front of the jumpsuit, another on the back of the full-length cape, something that would say

"America" to the world. He also designed a white leather belt four inches wide with four ovals in front, each with American eagles inside, all crafted in precious jewels.

In Los Angeles, meanwhile, "We Love Elvis" was being translated into the languages of countries where the concert was to be shown and the album sold; for this, RCA actually hired the Berlitz firm. Then Marty Pasetta had the phrases reproduced in neon and began designing a stage that was so large it would cover 3,500 of the 8,800 seats in what was (and still is) Honolulu's biggest auditorium.

January 1973 began with final fittings for his jewel-encrusted white costume and the shipment of tons of equipment from Los Angeles to Honolulu. Several days ahead of Elvis's departure, Pasetta and his crew flew over to begin filming big waves, misty mountain ridges, flowering trees, Diamond Head, and coconut palms—footage that would be edited into the satellite show to expand it to ninety minutes for telecast on the mainland.

At the same time, RCA's Rocky Laginestra decided that the album would be recorded in quadraphonic sound, the process that produced sound for four speakers rather than stereo's two.

Finally, on January 10, two days after quietly celebrating his thirty-eighth birthday with his new girlfriend, Linda Thompson, at Graceland, Elvis flew to the islands.

As more than a footnote, it should be acknowledged that Thompson, a former theater and English major at Memphis State University who represented Tennessee in the Miss USA pageant earlier in the year, contributed much to Elvis's good mood. She'd do anything to make him laugh, and usually she

Opposite, an *Advertiser* staff writer and a friend admire Elvis's cape at the Honolulu International Center.

succeeded. So when he arrived in Honolulu and checked into the Hilton Hawaiian Village, his mood was excellent.

Undoubtedly, this was abetted by his changed appearance. "[Previously] He was fat and he had a lot of problems with his stomach, which just quit working," one of his sidekicks, Sonny West, wrote in a book that was later to cause Elvis more pain. "His body just wasn't working. The pills were doing all the work, and yet when that television special came up, he dropped down to 165 pounds, thin as a rake, and more handsome than ten movie stars."

There were problems right away, one of them caused when Elvis gave the belt to his costume to actor Jack Lord. Belew, who was in Los Angeles, was called in a panic and told to make another, fast. "But we've used the last of the rubies!" he cried. "We'll have to get more from Europe."

A second problem arose when Elvis first saw the stage, which had individual risers, or platforms, for the members of his backup band, scattered widely.

"I'm sorry, sir," he told Pasetta, "but I like to have my boys with me. Isn't there some way we can keep everybody together?"

Pasetta crumbled and the risers were taken away.

The Joe Guercio Orchestra and backup singers, the Sweet Inspirations, who had worked for years behind Elvis in Vegas, J.D. Sumner and the Stamps, a gospel quartet whose leader went back to Elvis's beginnings in Memphis, and Kathy Westmoreland, whose high soprano was so much a part of his Vegas sound, arrived a few days before Elvis, filling an entire floor of the now much expanded hotel.

For the Honolulu media, Elvis became a daily story, much as he had when he was making his island movies. When he was touring, Elvis was usually in one place for no longer than it took to sleep for a few hours and then do a concert, leaving the next morning before the newspapers appeared. In Hawai'i he had a chance to read some of his press—and it contained nothing but the cheeriest praise. Honolulu's mayor Frank Fasi even declared the thirteenth, the day of the broadcast, "Elvis Presley Day."

As the sets were being constructed at the convention center, rehearsals were held quietly in the Hilton Hawaiian Dome, a geodesic structure fronting the hotel. Every day, Elvis wore a different outfit, including a long mink coat and white "Superfly" fedora, telling everyone he was "in disguise." When he wanted to go shopping, one of his boys made a call and the store was opened even at two o'clock in the morning. When Pasetta filmed his "arrival" at the Hilton helicopter pad, which became the show's opening, more than a thousand fans were present.

Elvis was back in the islands, and enjoying himself.

Thousands squeezed into the big auditorium for the dress rehearsal Friday night, many of them standing or sitting in the aisles. The performance was filmed as a matter of course, but there were technical problems.

On Saturday, the audience size was restricted, and to accommodate those who were turned away, the Colonel arranged to have plenty of entertainment outside—robots and clowns and high school bands. Now there were new technical problems. Pasetta and the engineer from Hollywood who came to record the album, Wally Heider, brought so much electrical equipment with them, they exhausted the local power source, and two hours before going on the air they picked up a hum from the lights.

A camera rises high above the audience to capture Elvis performing to a packed arena.

"We thought we'd lose the album and had to go scrounging to the navy to borrow thick lead sheets to baffle the hum," Pasetta recalled. "They came in, sirens blaring from Pearl Harbor, and we got them in place just minutes before we started broadcasting."

Earlier in the day, they also discovered a ten-minute error in the timing of the show. "We had it all timed out exactly in rehearsals," Pasetta said. "We'd whittled down the timings on Friday, apparently." When told about needing more material, Elvis merely nodded and sent his friend Charlie Hodge out with the titles of more songs for the orchestra. When a show was as loose as Elvis's was, with the repertoire often shifting midsong, last-minute changes meant nothing.

From the moment he walked onstage, announced by Richard Strauss's "Thus Spake Zarathustra" (as adapted for the movie *2001: A Space Odyssey* and readapted by Elvis's bandleader, Joe Guercio), the vast hall illuminated by the flashbulbs of thousands of Instamatics, the stage by hundreds of spotlights, Elvis was in total control.

He sang twenty-three songs, a wide assortment that swept up some of his distant past ("Love Me," "Blue Suede Shoes," "Long Tall Sally," "Johnny B. Goode," and "Hound Dog"), mixed deftly with newer material

JAN 14th HAWAII

1. SEE SEE RIDER
2. BURNING LOVE
3. SOMETHING
4. YOU GAVE A MOUTAIN
5. STEAMROLLER BLUES
6. ~~LOVE ME~~ MY WAY
7. LOVE ME
8. JOHN. y B GOOD
9. IT's OVER
10. BLUE SUEDE SHOES
11. I'M SO LONESOME I COULD CRY
12. I CAN'T STOP LOVING YOU
13. HOUND DOG
14. WHAT NOW MY LOVE
15. FEVER
16. WELCOME TO MY WORLD
17. SUSPICIOUS MINDS
18. I'LL REMEMBER YOU
19. LONG TALL SALLY-WHOLE LOTTA SHAKING GOIN ON
20. AMERICAN TRIOLGY
21. BIG HUNK OF LOVE
22. CAN'T HELP FALLING IN LOVE

Elvis always wrote out his proposed sequence of songs on a yellow legal pad before going on-stage and gave it to Charlie Hodge, who passed it along to the band members.

The Sunday Advertiser

Established July 2, 1856

THURSTON TWIGG-SMITH *President & Publisher*
GEORGE CHAPLIN *Editor-in-Chief*
BUCK BUCHWACH *Executive Editor*
JOHN GRIFFIN *Editorial Page Editor*
GENE HUNTER *Associate Editor*

HONOLULU, JANUARY 14, 1973

thanks to Elvis

Elvis Presley continues to be a great, good friend of Hawaii.

His two weekend benefit shows for the Kui Lee cancer research fund have produced over $75,000—bringing the total now in hand to over $115,000.

The fund was begun last summer by Advertiser columnist Eddie Sherman, with the full endorsement of the local chapter of the American Cancer Society, the Hawaii Medical Association and the University of Hawaii Medical School.

A letter from Sherman to Elvis' longtime manager, Col. Tom Parker, brought about the benefits, which met Parker's firm condition that no money could go for expenses, that every cent must reach the fund.

THIS IS THE second time that Elvis Presley has delivered for Hawaii in a big way.

The first, back in 1961, was also the result of an Advertiser project, the raising of funds to enable the completion of the U.S.S. Arizona memorial at Pearl Harbor.

The Advertiser had written to 1,600 other dailies across the country, appealing for December 7th editori-als asking funds for the Arizona project, on behalf of the Pacific War Memorial Commission. (The commission had raised some $250,000 but a like sum was still needed).

One of the editorials, appearing in a Los Angeles paper, was read by Colonel Parker, who phoned the editor of this newspaper and offered Elvis' services for a Honolulu benefit.

The conditions were the same as those which prevailed at the Honolulu shows. In that case, Bloch Arena was donated, as were the tickets, services by the ushers and all others involved.

Elvis raised $62,000 in one day performance and that stimulated Hawaii's congressional delegation to get enough additional Federal aid to finance the memorial.

DESPITE HIS enormous fame, Elvis Presley remains what writer Lloyd Shearer called some years ago: "One of the most considerate, well-mannered gentlemen" in the field of entertainment. He is still "warm, charming and friendly to everyone."

In 1973, as in 1961, Elvis and Colonel Parker, who shares his affection for Hawaii, deserve the Islands' great thanks and warmest aloha.

Right, Matt Esposito, manager of the Honolulu International Center, thanks Elvis, and so does the Sunday *Advertiser,* left.

("American Trilogy," "You Gave Me a Mountain," "Burning Love," "Suspicious Minds"), and a song that Frank Sinatra more or less made his own, "My Way," though it could be argued that Elvis had gone his own way, too. Plus, of course, Kui Lee's "I'll Remember You" and Elvis's local theme song, "Blue Hawaii."

Later, Peter Guralnick wrote in his biography *Careless Love: The Unmaking of Elvis Presley* that "there were musical highlights, for sure, but the overall atmosphere is even more stilted, and for all of his dramatic weight loss, Elvis appears strangely bloated, his expression glazed and unfocused. It is as if, in his Captain Marvel getup, his jewelry, his helmet of hair, Elvis has finally acceded to the need to be, simply, Elvis—there are no surprises, just effects."

Conforming to patterns long established, Elvis leaned down into the audience so fans could kiss him and encircle his neck with hugs and leis. Behind him, "We Love Elvis" blinked and flashed in a dozen languages. The backup band provided a thunderous beat, the audience a constant roar.

As he finished his traditional closing song, "Can't Help Falling in Love"—first recorded for *Blue Hawaii*—he dropped to one knee, right fist raised in triumph, his head bowed in simultaneous humility. Charlie Hodge picked up his jeweled cape and, as Elvis slowly stood, draped it gently on his shoulders. Elvis remained motionless with his head bowed for a moment and then took the $10,000 cape and sailed it into the audience like a Frisbee. Throwing up a hand in the Hawaiian "shaka" sign—thumb and little finger extended, the other fingers closed in the local sign of approval—he strode back into the offstage blackness to wait for the hall to clear.

A final five songs were then recorded in the empty auditorium for the expanded American telecast. Completing that, Elvis finally left the building.

In the limousine, the guys chorused, "Great show, boss, great show!"

Linda snuggled into his side and purred, "Personally, I was hoping you'd rip your pants."

The show went "on the air" by satellite at 12:30 in the morning Sunday. It was 7:30 p.m. Saturday in Tokyo and the show was the climax of a Japan-wide "Elvis Presley Week." The singer's popularity in that country was made clear when the station broadcasting the program announced the next day that Elvis had captured a 37.8 percent share of the audience in a highly competitive six-network market, breaking all Japanese television records.

The two shows also raised $75,000 for the Kui Lee Cancer Fund, $60,000 more than the goal set in November. In part, this was because the Colonel pressured prominent local personalities to contribute $1,000 apiece to watch the show—while many children got in for a penny.

The Sunday *Advertiser,* active in promoting the show, ran a lead editorial on January 14, 1973, saying, "Elvis Presley continues to be a great, good friend of Hawaii." The newspaper reminded readers that this was the second time that Elvis had "delivered for Hawaii in a big way," going on to recall the benefit for the *Arizona* Memorial a dozen years earlier. "In 1973, as in 1961, Elvis and Colonel Parker, who shares his affection for Hawaii, deserve the Islands' great thanks and warmest aloha."

Although the show cost approximately $2.5 million to produce, the most for any entertainment special to date, it was regarded as a huge success. The Colonel characteristically insisted that Elvis got not just a half-billion but a full billion viewers—a boast impossible to prove or disprove—and in April when the program was aired on NBC in the United States, it won a 57 percent share of those watching television and earned generally good reviews.

The album went onto the charts in early March and reached number one at the end of the month.

Elvis followed the show with a brief holiday, visiting the Oʻahu home of Jack Lord and his wife, Marie, giving the actor a gold-plated revolver and his wife an emerald and diamond ring. Elvis also said that *Hawaii Five-O* was one of his favorite shows and that he had, in fact, every episode on video. Elvis's belt was given an honored place on a wall in their home, mounted on black velvet and framed in black lacquer with a gold mat.

Kui Lee

Kui Lee was born in 1932 in Shanghai when his Hawaiian-Chinese-Scottish parents were touring the Far East along with other Hawaiian entertainers. His father was a falsetto singer, his mother a singer and a dancer. He started composing songs after the family returned to Hawai'i, as a teenager living in Papakōlea.

Following classes at Kamehameha and Roosevelt high schools, Lee served for two years in the U.S. Coast Guard and then duplicated his parents' separation from the islands, performing as a musician, singer, knife dancer, and sometime choreographer in Los Angeles, New York, and Puerto Rico. Reportedly, he wrote "I'll Remember You" when he left on one of his long mainland work trips, honoring his family— although the lyrics made it sound like a love song as well.

He returned to the islands for good in 1961, joining Don Ho at Honey's in Kāne'ohe, where the young Ho got his start as a singer. (Honey is Ho's mom.) Lee's voice wasn't strong, but he was given a feature spot in the small club's show. That's also when he showed his mentor some of his songs. In time, Ho experienced local success with "Ain't No Big Thing Bruddah," "The Days of My Youth," and "I'll Remember You."

By 1964, Lee had his own show at the legendary Queen's Surf on Waikīkī Beach and traveled to the neighbor islands, composing his plaintive "Lahainaluna" during an appearance in a hotel at Ka'anapali. His frisky tribute to canoeing, "One Paddle, Two Paddle," accompanied a revival in the ancient Hawaiian sport.

During all that time on the mainland, he listened carefully to rock and pop and jazz, and those elements were married to the English-language lyrics to make the music more western than Hawaiian. Yet his soul remained true to Hawai'i, and his music touched the new island state's pulse.

"Lee retained an essential Hawaiian quality," wrote George Kanahele in *Hawaiian Music and Musicians*, the encyclopedia of Hawaiian music. "In fact, Lee's Hawaiianness was the ultimate source of his identity and strength. His frustrations and joys, resentments and affections, were all tied to his efforts to protect and sustain his island heritage. He has been compared to James Dean, Hollywood's rebel without a cause, but Lee did have a cause: he protested against oligarchic rule and social pretense. His real image attracted a local folk hero cult who gathered at the old Queen's Surf at Waikīkī to listen to him sing and put down the 'phonies.' "

Lee composed some forty or so songs, mostly between 1956 and 1961, when he was on the mainland. Since he lived less than six

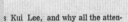

years after his return to Hawai'i, and suffered from throat cancer the last two years of his life, his output was limited.

He died on December 3, 1966, in Tijuana, Mexico, where he'd gone for laetrile treatment, banned by the Food and Drug Administration in the United States. He was buried at sea off Waikīkī Beach six days later in a ceremony that drew thousands of fans. He was just thirty-four.

Kui Lee's songs remain a part of nearly every Hawaiian singer's repertoire, and his own recordings continue to be repackaged. He's also remembered every year at the Nā Hōkū Hanohano Awards, the Hawaiian music industry's version of the Grammy show, when a contemporary performer is given the Kui Lee Lifetime Achievement Award.

CHAPTER 7

Elvis in Hawai'i

The 1973 satellite concert was Elvis's last performance in Hawai'i and, tragically, the final big challenge of his career. In the four years between his "Aloha from Hawaii" concert and his final visit to Hawai'i in 1977, Elvis's career and health fell precipitously.

The recording sessions, regular Vegas engagements, and endless tours all became difficult; many were cancelled, and several were ridiculed by critics. "It's Elvis at his most indifferent, uninterested, and unappealing," the *Hollywood Reporter* said following a Vegas opening in 1973, only months after the triumph in Hawai'i.

His intake of prescription drugs accelerated, resulting in two emergency hospitalizations. His divorce from Priscilla turned acrimonious, and by the time it was finalized, Linda was beginning to lose her patience, leaving him in 1976.

The money kept pouring in and Elvis spent it, lavishly and often frivolously, on jewelry, cars, guns, and a second airplane; he made as much money as an Arabian prince, and spent as much as two.

Meanwhile, RCA was forced to release what were called "grab-bag" albums, collections of whatever previously unreleased material they could find, followed by *The Legendary Performer* in two volumes and *The Sun Sessions,* anthologies of old material. Lawsuits were filed, some claiming Elvis's patrimony, others charging his sidekicks with violence. He fired some of his boys, and three of them retaliated in a tattletale book, *Elvis: What Happened?,* ghostwritten by an editor of a gossip tabloid, making Elvis sound like an out-of-control, gun-crazed, cop-obsessed, drug-addicted spiritual kook. Their arguments were credible.

Elvis's last holiday in the islands was in March 1977, four months before his death. By now, the islands offered a familiar escape. Only Las Vegas competed for his holiday attention, and there, he seldom strayed from his spacious suite other than to view another entertainer's performance. In Hawai'i, he could relax and wander more freely. And where the dry desert climate of Nevada is unwelcoming, insisting you remain inside, Hawai'i offers a warm, caressing comfort zone that insists you go outdoors to experience it.

For this last holiday—undertaken after he drew up a new will, leaving everything to his father—it was decided that he and his party would leave from Oakland, California, because

Opposite, Elvis takes a break from playing touch football on Lanikai Beach with Larry Geller, *right*, his hairdresser and spiritual advisor, and his cousin Billy Smith's wife Jo, *foreground.*

Elvis relaxes in front of his Lanikai house with Ginger Alden, *left,* and her sister Rosemary; his step-brother David Stanley has his back to the camera, *right.*

it was two-hundred miles closer to Honolulu than Los Angeles. He was taking the plane he named for his daughter, the *Lisa Marie,* and wanted every margin of safety in fuel loading.

Not one to do anything by halves, however, Elvis took thirty-one friends with him, including his new girlfriend, Ginger Alden, twenty, a former Miss Traffic Safety and current Miss Mid-South, reserving rooms in the Hilton Hawaiian Village hotel and renting a house from a Honolulu physician, on the beach in Lanikai, about half an hour's drive from Waikīkī. With a view of several small off-shore islands, this neighborhood was regarded as one of the most relaxed and, simultaneously, one of the most prestigious.

The beach house was for Elvis and Ginger and her two sisters, plus one bodyguard. The others stayed in the hotel and came over during the day or joined Elvis on his occasional public forays. One evening, they were sneaked into the Polynesian Cultural Center—the location for many scenes in *Paradise, Hawaiian Style*—and other times, he took Ginger and her sisters and some of the others

to one of the small shopping centers near the beach house. There, he greeted fans warmly, bought presents for everyone, and on one occasion, paid the bill for a stranger who was making a purchase for his wife.

Most of the ten days in Hawai'i were spent close to home, sitting on the beach in sunglasses and a floppy cloth hat, playing Ping-Pong at the house, or touch football on the narrow strand beside the lapping surf. Those who had been with Elvis for some time said later that his health improved during the vacation, that his color was better, his eyes brighter and clearer.

"Elvis Presley loved Hawai'i," says Tom Moffatt, the deejay closest to the Presley-Parker camp over the years, "from the moment he landed here in 1957, through all his concerts, three movies, and many vacation getaways. And Hawai'i loved Elvis just as much. These islands have always been a godsend for celebrities, because people here respect their privacy. Once away from the tourist areas, Elvis could relax and go to the beach just like everyone else. For someone who was famous worldwide, this was a great—and very unappreciated—change."

Joe Esposito, Elvis's major domo over the years, agreed. In *Good Rockin' Tonight* (virtually everyone who ever knew Elvis wrote a book) he said that "Elvis loved Hawai'i. The weather was fabulous, and the people treated him with respect. Unlike Mainland fans, who hounded him wherever he went, the Hawaiians left Elvis alone."

There was another observer who hadn't seen Elvis in some time, and he was shocked by what he saw on this final visit to the islands. This was Kalani Simerson, a onetime Waikīkī performer who operated a successful limousine service. He'd known Elvis and had worked for him since the early 1960s, when Elvis made his first films in Hawai'i. The last time he'd seen Elvis was at the satellite show. As before, Kalani was called to make some of the travel arrangements for this visit, and because of his long-standing friendship, he was invited to join Elvis on the beach socially.

"We played football," Kalani said later, "and it was sad, very sad. Elvis was overweight and just unable to function normally. I guess it was all that medication they said he took. Somebody'd throw him the ball and he'd catch it and start running and he couldn't stop. He just wasn't able to control his own body. One time he ran right into a cyclone fence and cut his hand."

On the fourteenth day, Elvis got some

A first-day cover issued by the post office on Elvis's birthday, the day of the first sale of a U.S. commemorative stamp honoring Elvis in 1993; the drawing is of the Graceland gates.

sand in his eyes and abruptly the vacation was ended.

Five days after that he was back on tour again.

*****

Click on to www.elvisinhawaii.com, a Web page emanating from the Netherlands, or walk down Kalākaua Avenue to see one of Waikīkī's two Elvis impersonators and it's clear that Elvis is still alive and well, at least in the fiftieth state. Charlie Ross may still be trying to get a plaque crediting Elvis's contribution to the U.S.S. *Arizona* Memorial, but there was no surprise when a store in Waikīkī's International Market Place sold only Elvis memorabilia for a few years, or that *Elvis Monthly* magazine, published in England, for many years ran charter tours to the islands for British fans.

Island residents might have been startled when it was revealed that Elvis's daughter, Lisa Marie, became engaged, in 2000, to John Oszajca, a musician from Kailua seven years younger than she was, but there is no amazement when Elvis's name and photo appear in the daily press on anniversaries of his birth and death and the dedication of the *Arizona* Memorial. Elvis is remembered worldwide, of course, but in Hawai'i, the memories seem more vivid, more personal, just as they do in Memphis but not in Las Vegas or Hollywood, where he spent comparatively much more time. Thus, Hawai'i was, in a

OFFICE OF THE MAYOR
CITY AND COUNTY OF HONOLULU

PROCLAMATION

WHEREAS, though the Kingdom of Hawaii was governed by many monarchs, the only King who ruled the State of Hawaii was Elvis Presley; and

WHEREAS, Elvis returned the love of the people of Hawaii with genuine aloha; and

WHEREAS, like the pied piper of old, the King of Rock 'n Roll enticed countless visitors to our islands through his many films set here in paradise; and

WHEREAS, Elvis donated his time and talent to many local charities, notably his star appearance in a 1961 fundraising concert which garnered over $62,000 for the construction of the U.S.S. Arizona Memorial, dedicated to those servicemen who lost their lives in the tragic Pearl Harbor attack; and

WHEREAS, he again demonstrated his generosity in his "Aloha from Hawaii" concert which was broadcast live to 49 countries and raised $75,000 for the Kui Lee Cancer Fund; and

WHEREAS, even after his death, Elvis' music lives on and brings joy to thousands in Hawaii and around the world; and

WHEREAS, fans and loved ones will gather in Graceland to commemorate his death and celebrate his life; and

WHEREAS, Bruno Hernandez, who at four years of age is Elvis' youngest impersonator, will travel to Tennessee to perform in a special tribute to the Rock 'n Roll legend,

NOW, THEREFORE, I, FRANK F. FASI, Mayor of the City and County of Honolulu, do hereby proclaim August 12-18, 1990, as

ELVIS PRESLEY TRIBUTE WEEK

in the City and County of Honolulu, extend congratulations to Bruno for this honored invitation, and encourage the citizens of Honolulu to remember Elvis' special contributions at this time.

IN WITNESS WHEREOF, I have hereunto set my hand and caused the Seal of the City and County of Honolulu to be affixed.

Done this 31st day of July, 1990, in Honolulu, Hawaii.

FRANK F. FASI, Mayor
City and County of Honolulu

On July 3, 1990, Mayor Frank Fasi proclaimed August 12–18, 1990, as Elvis Presley Tribute Week.

sense, his second home, even in the minds of residents.

The commercial connection between Elvis and the islands remained, too. Charlie Hodge published a book of photographs taken on the final Hawai'i holiday and for a time he traveled what was then a burgeoning Elvis Presley convention circuit, selling the book and posing for pictures with fans, who paid five dollars for the privilege.

Similarly, Stella Stevens, Elvis's leading lady in *Girls! Girls! Girls!*, wrote a novel, *Razzle Dazzle*, whose main character was inspired by Elvis, and several actors and actresses who were in his Hawai'i films sold autographed publicity stills on the Internet; the autographs were not Elvis's, but those of the now forgotten actresses.

There was also something called "Elvis's Hawaiian Hideaway," marketed as a vacation rental on the Internet by Hawaiian Island Getaways. This was a five-and-a-half-acre estate on O'ahu's North Shore at Pūpūkea, once owned by Maurice Sullivan, founder of Hawai'i's Foodland supermarket chain and the man who brought McDonald's to the islands. Elvis stayed in the house only once, preferring the doctor's house in Lanikai.

Videos, CDs, and tapes of his island concerts and movies were offered on hundreds of Web sites and stocked in stores worldwide, eventually going "gold" and then "platinum," the ultimate in music sales. All of Elvis's island music has sold better since he died

than it did when he was alive (a phenomenon common in popular music throughout much of the world; cynics often call a musician's early death a "good career move").

In 1989, Tom Moffatt and Ron Jacobs, who maintained contact with the Colonel over the years, flew to Las Vegas for his seventy-third birthday, taking with them a proclamation signed by Governor John Waihe'e, saying the memory of Elvis "is alive in Hawai'i. It lives on in more than his music, for the Colonel and Elvis gave to our islands a very special aloha." Calling Elvis "a great ambassador and troubadour for Hawai'i," he closed by saying, "Thank you, Colonel, for it all." In 1997, when the Colonel died at age 87, Moffatt and Jacobs returned to Nevada as honorary pallbearers.

Of course, there were Elvis sightings, too—extending long after his death, when island residents reported seeing the last Hawaiian king eating a hamburger at the Manoa Marketplace, for instance, and standing alone on Waikīkī Beach on a full moon night. There was even a book published in 1988, titled *Is Elvis Alive?*, that said he had faked his death and was living in the islands as John Burrows, the name of one of his movie characters.

And why not?

Dreams come true in blue Hawai'i.

Elvis said that.

Why not fantasies, too?

How Much Is That Hound Dog in the Window?

Elvis died in his Graceland home of a heart attack caused by an overdose of prescription drugs on August 16, 1977, just five months after his holiday in Lanikai. Since then, his crown as the King of Rock and Roll has remained firmly in place.

In addition to the rereleased and repackaged tapes and CDs and videocassettes and

DVDs, a huge market for Elvis memorabilia materialized, commanding prices that astonished everyone except Elvis fans who were willing to pay so much for what was, often, so little. Many of these "collectibles" reflected Elvis's long commitment to the islands.

Because Elvis was extraordinarily generous, giving so many gifts both to friends and people he didn't know, there were at the time of his death perhaps thousands of items that carried the Elvis imprint, many of which changed hands in private transactions, always for more money than their original worth. Countless more were sold in auction, some of the most interesting from Colonel Parker's

Left, papier-mâché leis like this one, with a cardboard medallion attached—Elvis's face and facsimile autograph on one side, a plug for *Blue Hawaii* on the other—were a commonplace promotional item in 1961; this lei is displayed with an autographed Hilton Hawaiian Village cocktail napkin signed 3/28/61. *Right,* on the napkin, Elvis wrote, "To Dan and Maria Aloha from Elvis Presley."

vast collection and from the Elvis Presley Estate.

Many of the items were sold at an auction held by Lisa Marie Presley at the MGM Grand Hotel in Las Vegas in 1999 to raise money for a homeless shelter. Organized by Guernsey's, a New York–based auction house, even so mundane a "collectible" as an accounting of Elvis's earnings from *Blue Hawaii*, on the Colonel's stationery, along with checks from the William Morris Agency and Paramount Pictures—taken from the Colonel's files— were valued together at between $1,200 and $1,600, and sold for $2,750. Colonel Parker's soundtrack LP silver record from the Record Industry Association of America, mounted and framed, connoting a million records sold, went for $3,500. A ticket to the 1961 *Arizona* Memorial concert sold for $3,750. And fifty-four pages of itemized hotel receipts from the Hilton Hawaiian Village during the month of January 1973 got $4,500.

No one knows the true value of the "set list" for the songs Elvis planned to include in the *Arizona* Memorial concert, written in Elvis's hand and mailed to one of his most ardent fans, Gary Pepper (a young man confined to a wheelchair, to whom Elvis sent regular checks). The present owner, a Memphis resident, says his brother, also an Elvis fan, bought the list and the envelope it came in (see page 24) for $1,200 in 1979. The present owner and the auction house through which he's offering it, Entertainment Rarities in Los Angeles, estimates $13,000.

There seems to be no limit.

Items reasonably regarded as worthless at the time of their initial distribution were morphed Midas-like into gold after Elvis's death. Paper flower leis handed out by the hundreds, maybe thousands, promoting *Blue Hawaii,* now were sold at auction for $65 apiece, the only thing differentiating them from almost identical leis sold in Waikīkī today for under a dollar being a small paper medallion, a photo of Elvis in an aloha shirt on one side, a plug for the movie on the other.

The Pan Am flight brochure that Elvis autographed for a fellow passenger on the flight to Hawai'i in 1961 had a price tag of

Another auction item, an airline brochure autographed by Elvis on board a flight to Honolulu in 1961; correcting the name, he added a P.S. Sorry about that!

A shirt worn by Elvis in *Paradise, Hawaiian Style*, 1966. This shirt sold at auction for $10,500 two years ago.

$800–1,200. A lei and an autographed Hilton Hawaiian Village hotel napkin together were valued at $2,500. A Sotheby's catalog listed a blue linen shirt that Elvis wore in *Paradise, Hawaiian Style,* estimating its value at between $7,000 and $9,000; it sold for $10,500.

What's the most expensive Elvis item associated with Hawai'i ever sold? It might be one from the Guernsey's sale in 1999. So much stuff was offered at this auction the catalog was printed in three volumes. The Eagle Cape worn by the King during his "Aloha from Hawaii" satellite show went for $85,000.

Index

Page numbers in bold indicate photographs.

Elvis with Donna Butterworth

Elvis at *Arizona* Memorial press conference

Joan Blackman and Elvis

F

G

H

I

The Jordanaires

Elvis in *Paradise, Hawaiian Style*

Joan Blackman and Elvis